BECOME LEGACY CREATIONS

MOTIVATIONAL GOAL PLANNER

BECOME THE LEGACY

YOU WERE MADE TO BE

SELF EVALUATION

TALENTS

HABITS

AMBITIONS

LIKES

What aligns to my purpose?

GOALS

IMPACTS

STRENGTHS

LIKES

TO KNOW WHAT YOU LIKE WILL HELP YOU UNDERSTAND YOUR PASSION

WHAT DOES HAPPINESS MEAN TO ME?

MY LIKES

WHAT EXCITES ME THE MOST ABOUT LIFE?

MY DISLIKES

NOTES

"We all die. The goal isn't to live forever, the goal is to create something that will." -Chuck Palahniuk

TALENTS

USE YOUR TALENTS TO THE GREATEST ADVANTAGE AND YOU CAN CHANGE THE WORLD

WHAT MAKES ME UNIQUE?

MY TALENTS

WHAT IS MY SUPERPOWER?

COMPLIMENTS

NOTES

"We make a living by what we get. We make a life by what we give." -Winston Churchill

HABITS

YOUR HABITS SHAPE WHO YOU ARE AND LEA
YOU TO YOUR ULTIMATE DESTINY

HOW DO YOU IMAGINE A DAILY ROUTINE?

GOOD HABITS

WHAT WASTES MY TIME THE MOST?

BAD HABITS

NOTES

"The bad news is time flies by. The good news is you're the pilot." -Michael Altshuler

AMBITIONS

KNOWING WHAT MOTIVATES YOU WILL GIVE YOU THE ENERGY TO PURSUE YOUR DREAMS

HOW IS MY LEVEL OF SELF-DISCIPLINE?

DESIRES

WHAT ARE MY MOTIVATIONS AND MORALS?

WANTS

NOTES

"If you are working on something that you really care about, you don't have to be pushed. The vision pulls you." -Steve Jobs

GOALS

ACCOMPLISHING YOUR GOALS A LITTLE AT A TIME DEVELOPS YOUR GROWTH

HOW DO I ENVISION MYSELF TO BE?

GOALS

HOW DO I ENHANCE MY SELF-IMPROVEMENT?

DREAMS

NOTES

"I think goals should never be easy, they should force you to work, even if they are uncomfortable at the time." -Michael Phelps

STRENGTHS

IDENTIFYING YOUR STRENGTHS AND WEAKNESSES GIVES YOU POWER TO DEFEAT YOUR BATTLES

WHAT DO I BELIEVE SETS ME APART FROM EVERYONE?

STRENGTHS

WHAT ARE THE CHALLENGES I FACE FOR GROWTH?

WEAKNESSES

NOTES

"Never bend your head. Always hold it high. Look the world straight in the eye." -Helen Keller

IMPACTS

THE IMPACT YOU LEAVE FOR THE WORLD IS THE LEGACY YOU CREATED

WHAT ARE THE QUALITIES I LOOK FOR IN A LEADER?

INFLUENCES

WHO DO I VIEW AS THE MOST INFLUENTIAL IN THE WORLD?

VALUES

NOTES

"Leaders think and talk about the solutions. Followers think and talk about the problem." -Brian Tracy

BRAINSTORMING

IDEA

THE SPARK, THE INNOVATION, THE CHANGE

WHAT IS THE MOST EFFICIENT WAY TO RECORD MY IDEAS?

DESIGNS

WHICH IDEAS ARE THE MOST IMPACTFUL FOR MY DREAMS?

IDEAS

NOTES

"It is often the small steps, not the giant leaps, that bring about the most lasting change." - Queen Elizabeth

PLAN

MAKING A PLAN GIVES US THE DIRECTION TO OUR SUCCESS

WHAT WILL PREPARE MY STEPS TO MY GOALS?

PLANS

HOW WILL I EXECUTE MY PLAN?

ACTIONS

NOTES

"You don't have to be great to start, but you have to start to be great." -Zig Ziglar

VISION

A VISION LIVES WITHIN YOU, YOU MUST LET THE WORLD SEE YOUR VISION

WHAT IS THE IMPACT I WANT TO HAVE IN THE WORLD?

VISIONS

HOW WOULD I DESCRIBE GREATNESS?

PERSPECTIVES

NOTES

"Do what you can with all you have, wherever you are." -Theodore Roosevelt

LEARN

YOU MUST ALWAYS BE A STUDENT AS LEARNING IS THE STRONGEST FORM OF GROWTH

WHERE MUST I SEEK MY RESEARCH?

TRAININGS

WHO WOULD BE MOST BENEFICIAL AS A MENTOR?

RESOURCES

NOTES

"We cannot solve our problems with the same thinking we used to create them." -Albert Einstein

CREATE

CREATING MAKES US WHO WE ARE AND OPE
THE DOOR TO NEW PERSPECTIVES

HOW SHOULD I EXPRESS WHO I AM?

PROJECTS

WHAT WAYS WILL HELP ME BUILD MY POTENTIAL?

PURSUITS

NOTES

"Everything you can imagine is real" -Pablo Picasso

PROBLEM

IDENTIFYING YOUR STRUGGLES REACHING YOUR GOALS WILL HELP YOU OVERCOME THEM

WHAT ARE THE CONSTANT BATTLES I FACE?

PROBLEMS

WHAT IS MOST EFFECTIVE TO LEARN FROM MISTAKES?

HARDSHIPS

NOTES

"I am not a product of my circumstances. I am a product of my decisions." -Stephen Covey

NETWORK

HOW YOU VALUE AND BUILD THE PEOPLE SURROUNDING YOU IS YOUR STRENGTH

HOW DO I ENGAGE WITH PEOPLE?

NETWORKS

AM I ACTIVELY SUPPORTING OTHERS?

CONNECTIONS

NOTES

"Your network is your net worth." -Porter Gale

GOAL MAPPING

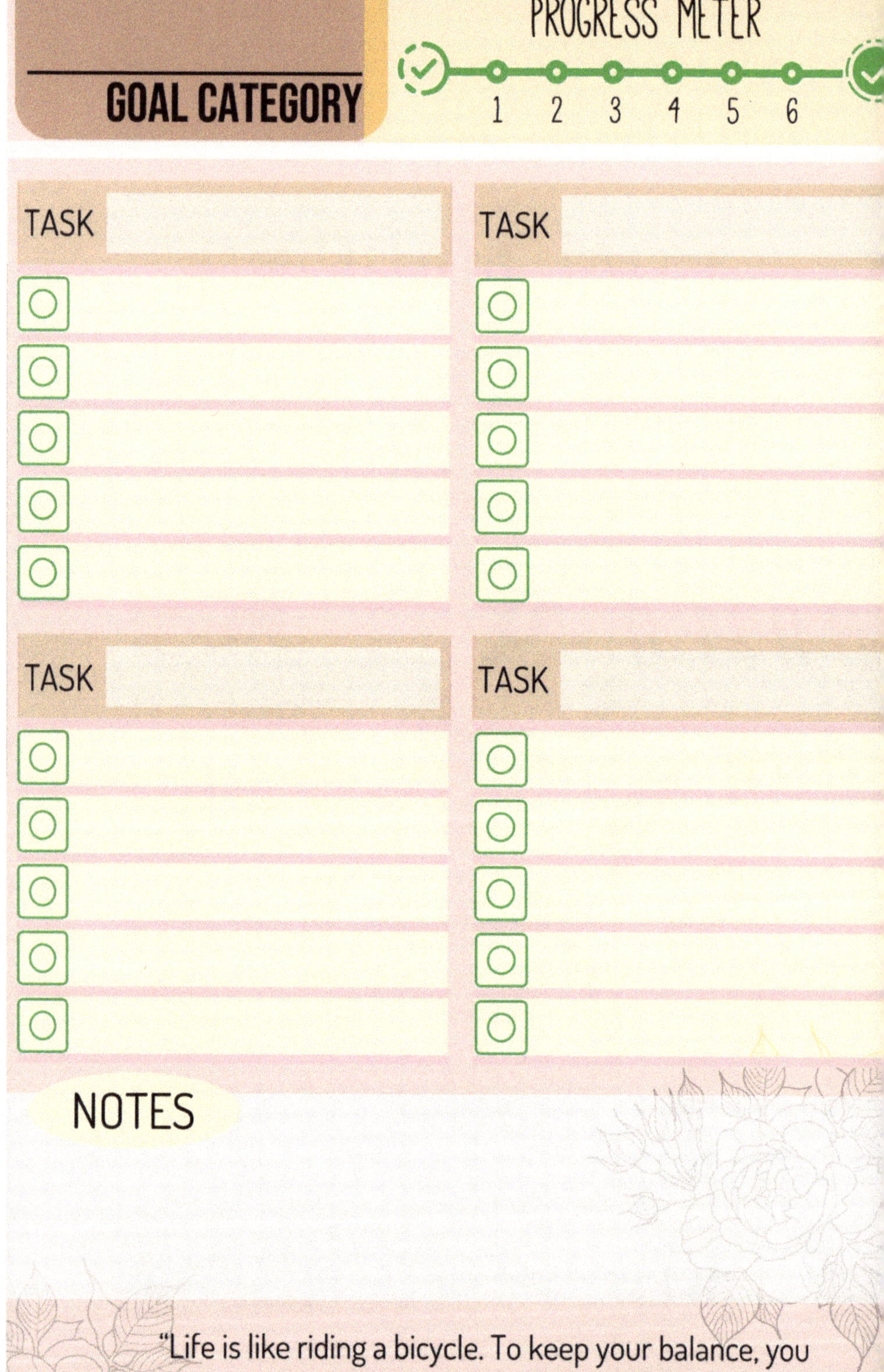

"Life is like riding a bicycle. To keep your balance, you must keep moving." -Albert Einstein

TART DATE:

DUE DATE:

TYPES OF GOALS

Finacial Health Fitness Personal Career Social

ASK

TASK

WHAT HAVE I LEARNED?

WHAT AM I PRIORITIZING?

NOTES

Never limit yourself because of others' limited imagination; never limit others because of your own limited imagination." -Mae Jemison

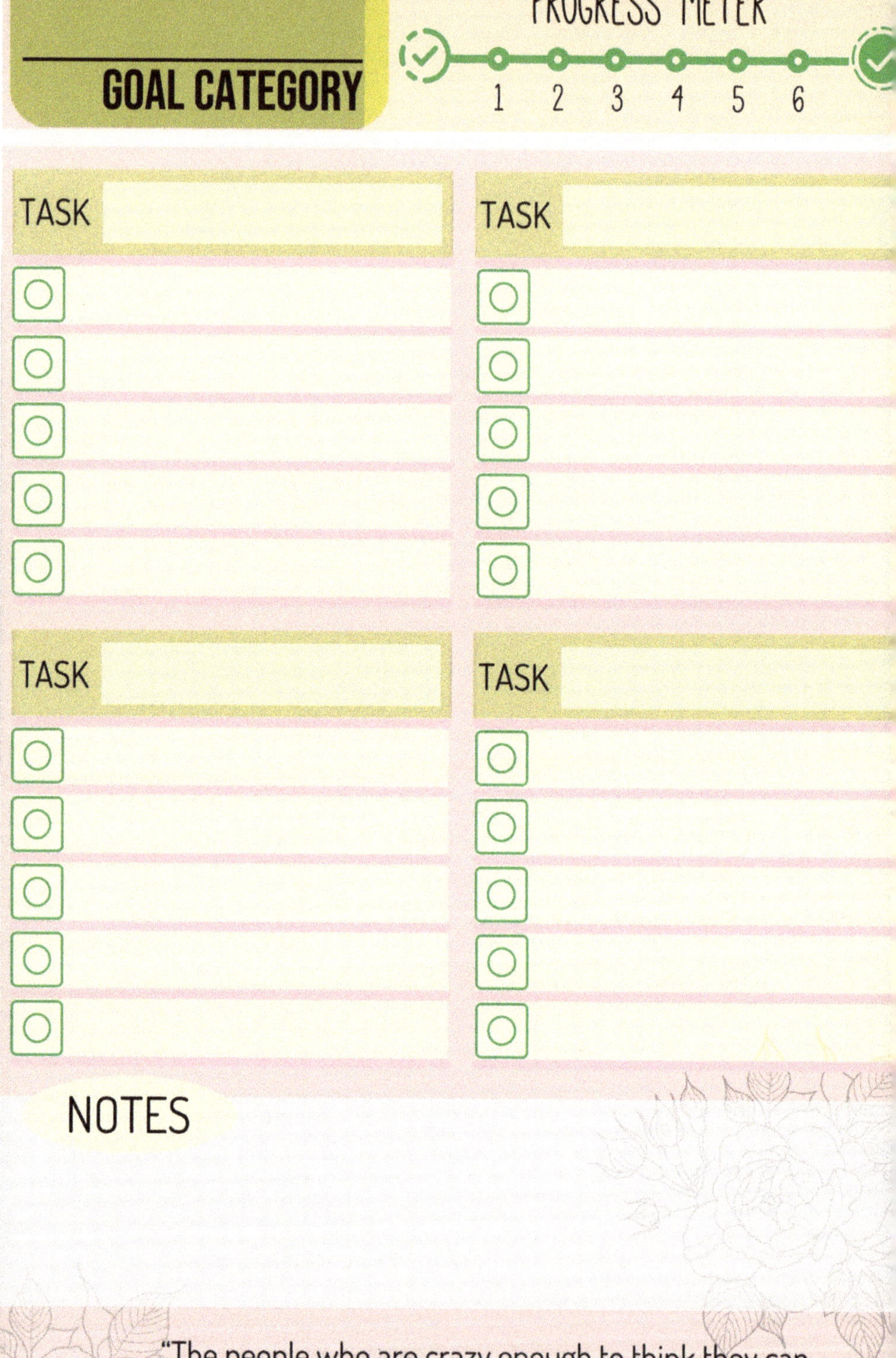

"The people who are crazy enough to think they can change the world are the ones who do." – Steve Jobs

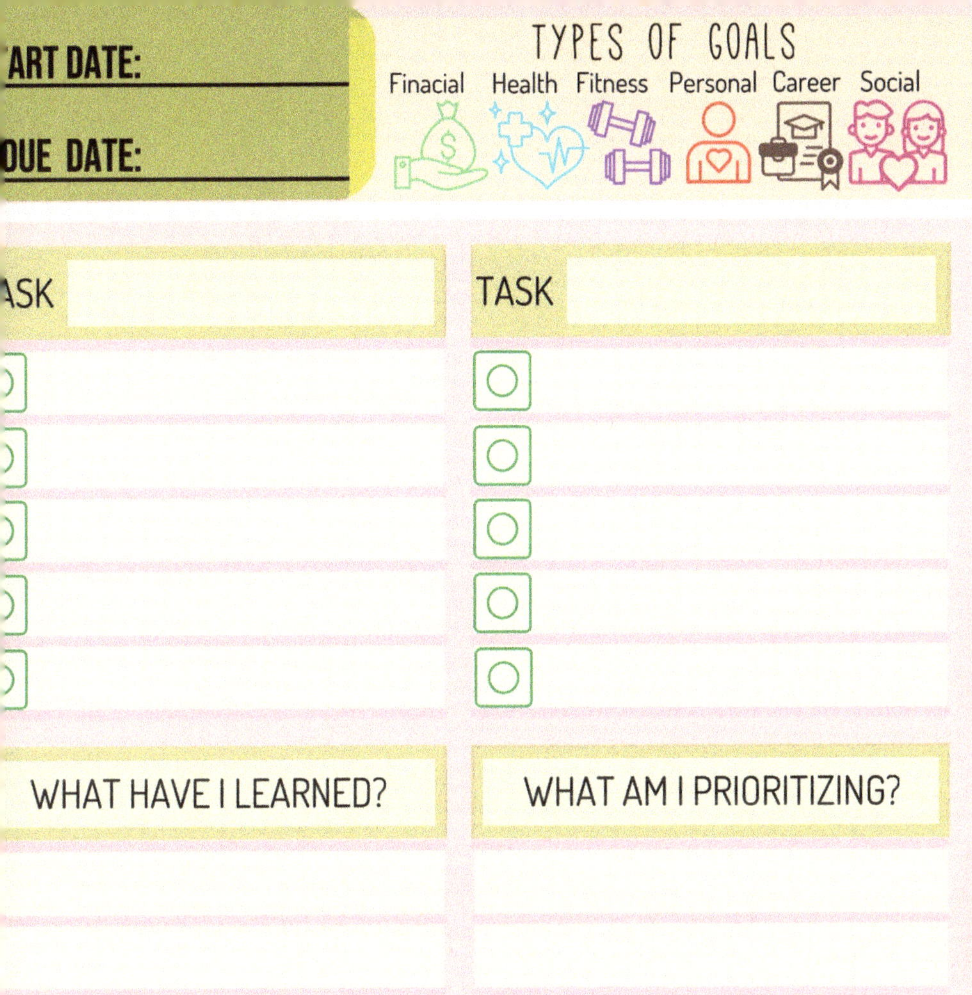

ART DATE:

DUE DATE:

TYPES OF GOALS

Finacial Health Fitness Personal Career Social

ASK	
☐	
☐	
☐	
☐	
☐	

TASK	
☐	
☐	
☐	
☐	
☐	

WHAT HAVE I LEARNED?

WHAT AM I PRIORITIZING?

NOTES

"Once you replace negative thoughts with positive ones, you'll start having positive results." - Willie Nelson

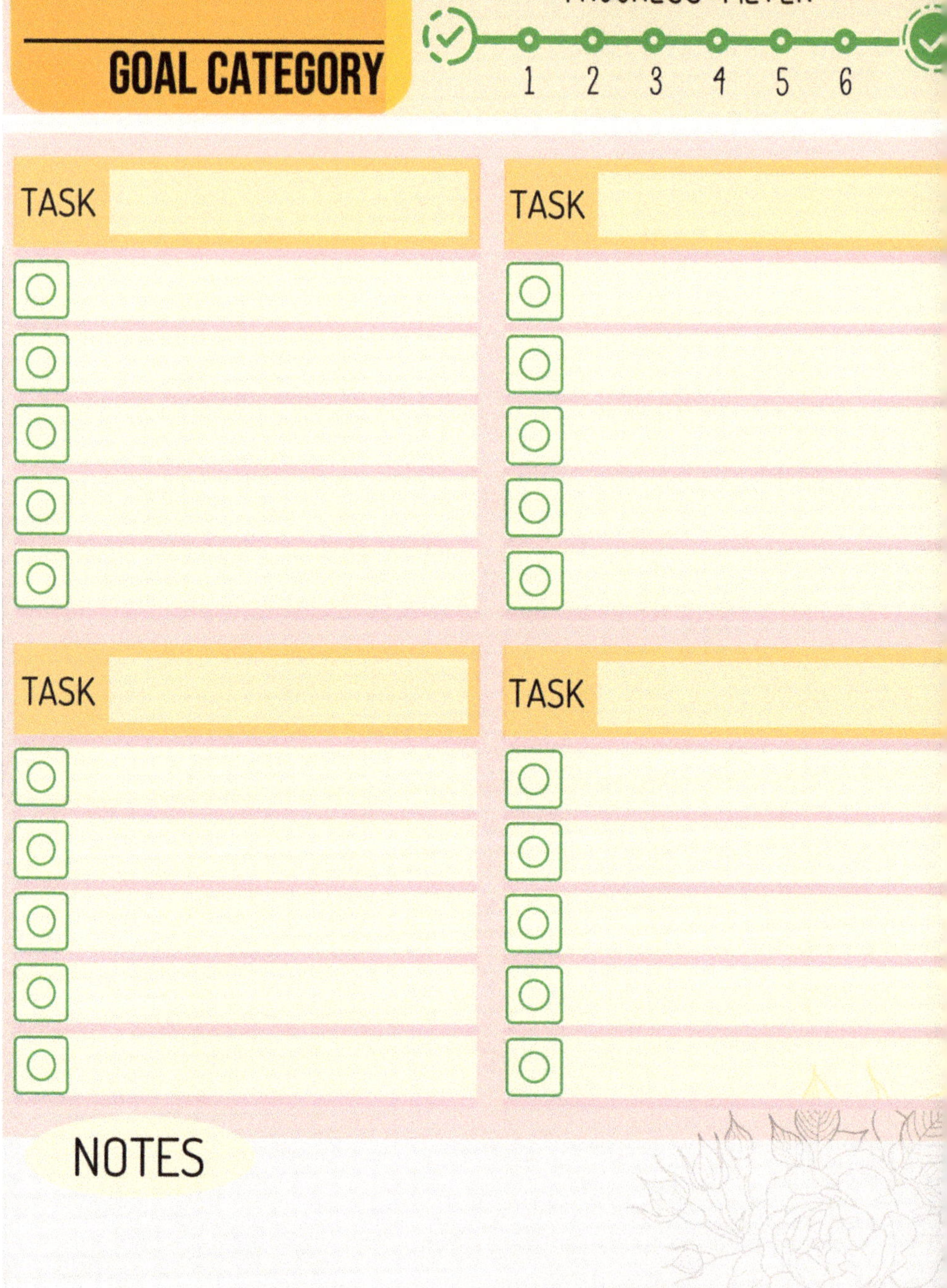

NOTES

"Optimism is a happiness magnet. If you stay positive, good things and good people will be drawn to you."- Mary Lou Retton

TART DATE:
DUE DATE:
TYPES OF GOALS
Finacial
Health
Fitness
Personal
Career
Social
ASK
TASK
WHAT HAVE I LEARNED?
WHAT AM I PRIORITIZING?
NOTES
“You do not find the happy life. You make it.”
- Camilla Eyring Kimball

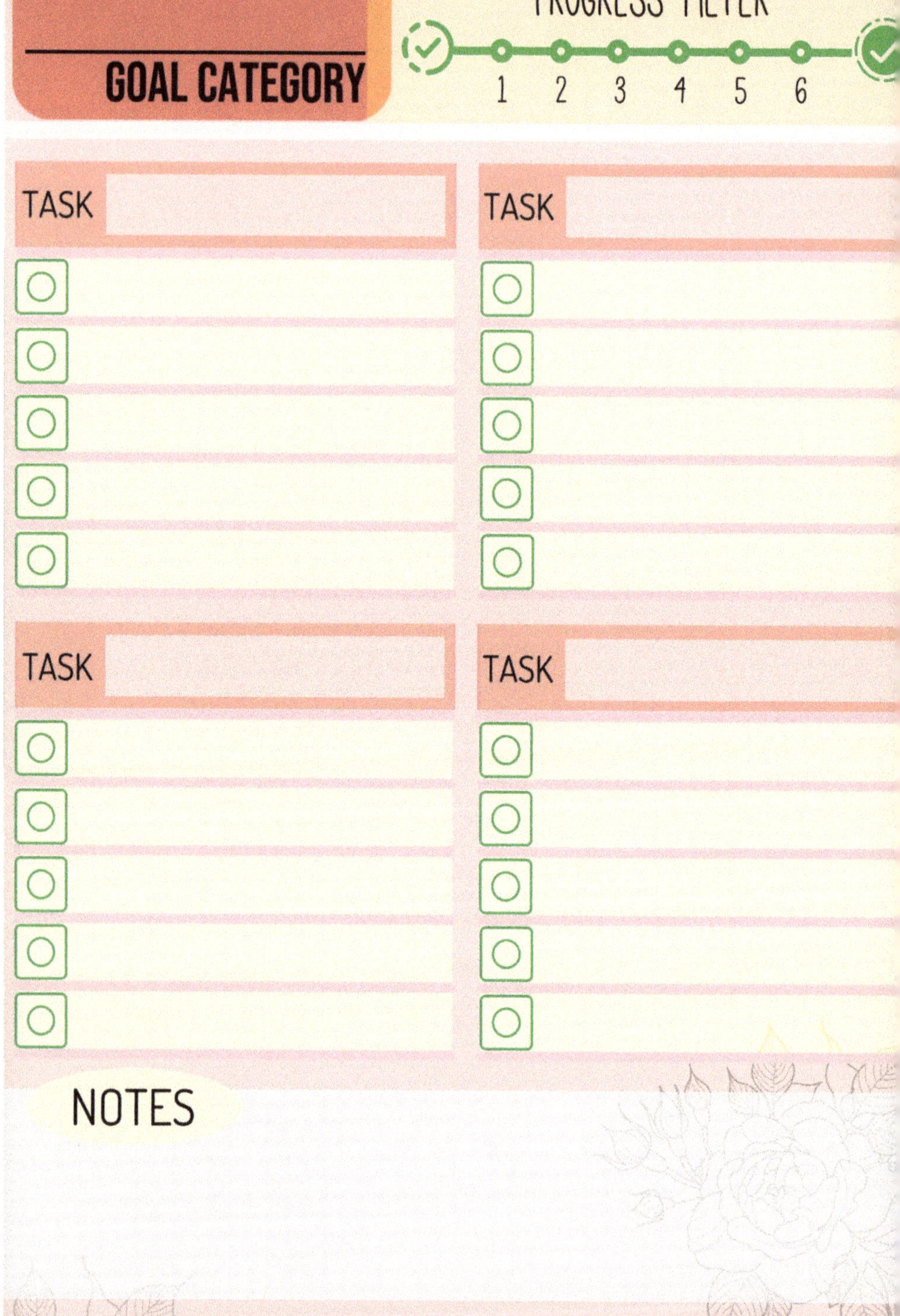

"If you want to lift yourself up, lift up someone else."
-Booker T. Washington

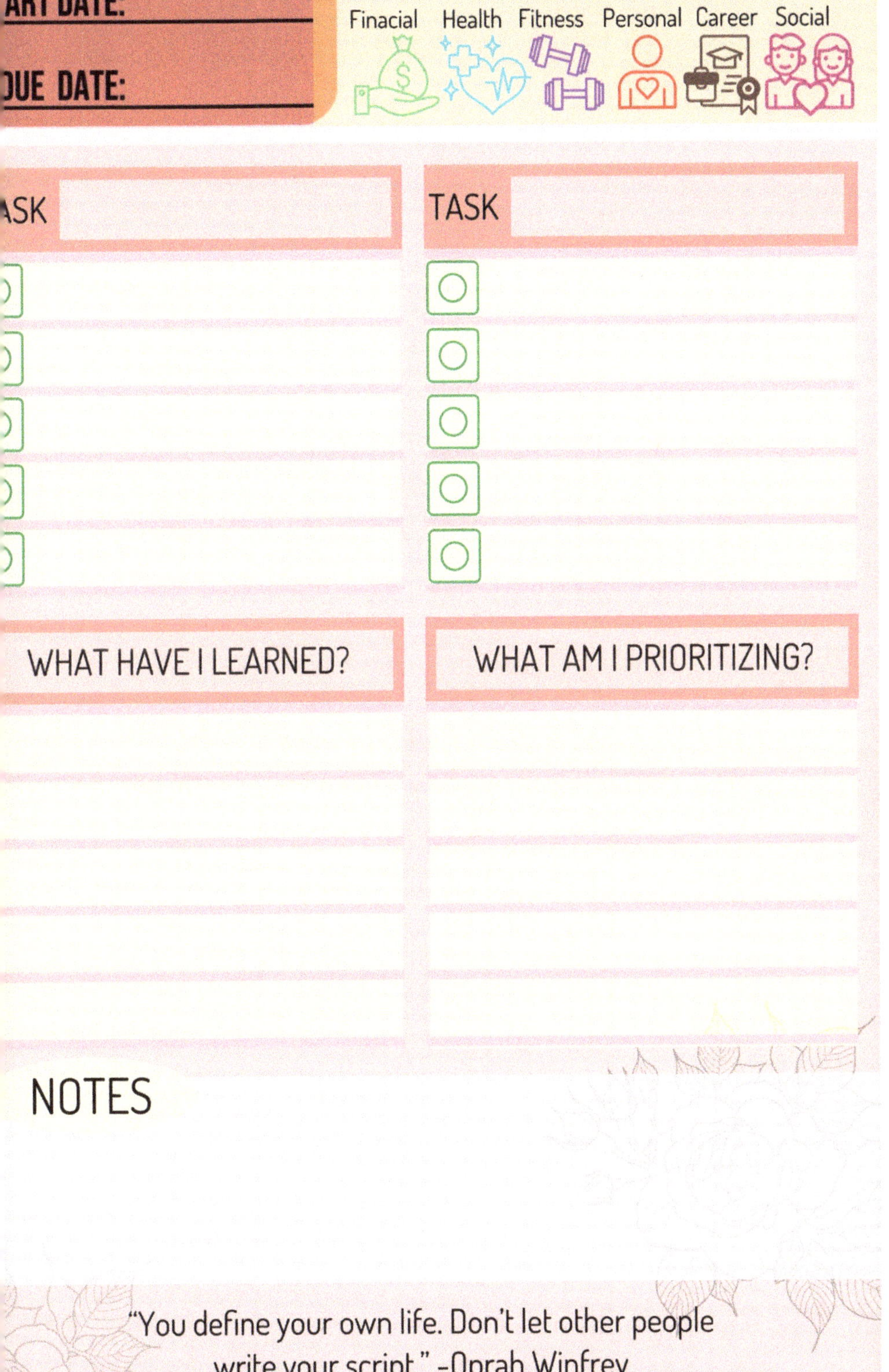
ART DATE:
UE DATE:
TYPES OF GOALS
Finacial
Health
Fitness
Personal
Career
Social
ASK
TASK
WHAT HAVE I LEARNED?
WHAT AM I PRIORITIZING?
NOTES
"You define your own life. Don't let other people write your script." -Oprah Winfrey

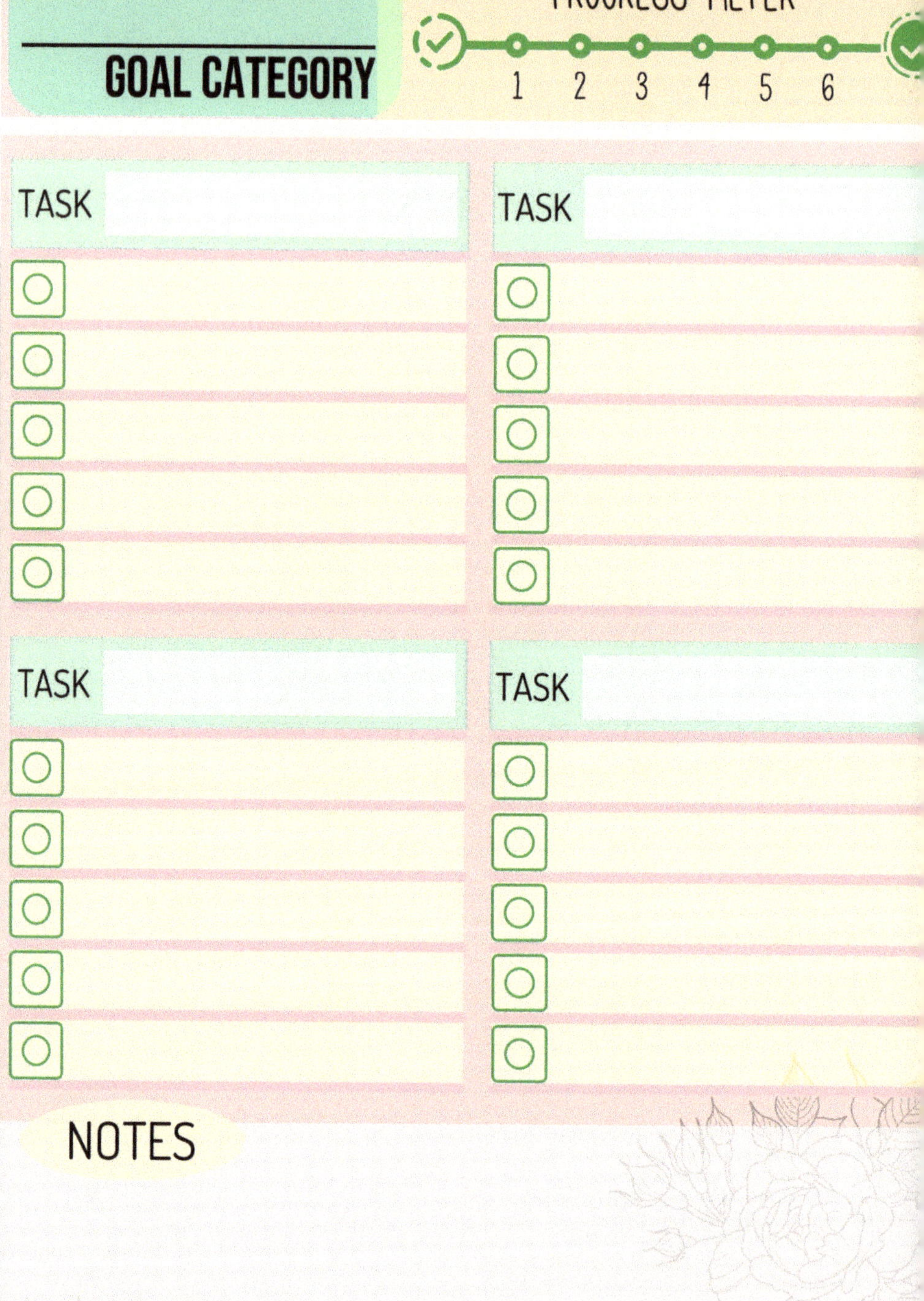

NOTES

"Remember that the airplane takes off against the wind, not with it." –Henry Ford

TART DATE:

DUE DATE:

TYPES OF GOALS

Finacial Health Fitness Personal Career Social

ASK

TASK

WHAT HAVE I LEARNED?

WHAT AM I PRIORITIZING?

NOTES

"A person who never made a mistake never tried anything new." -Albert Einstein

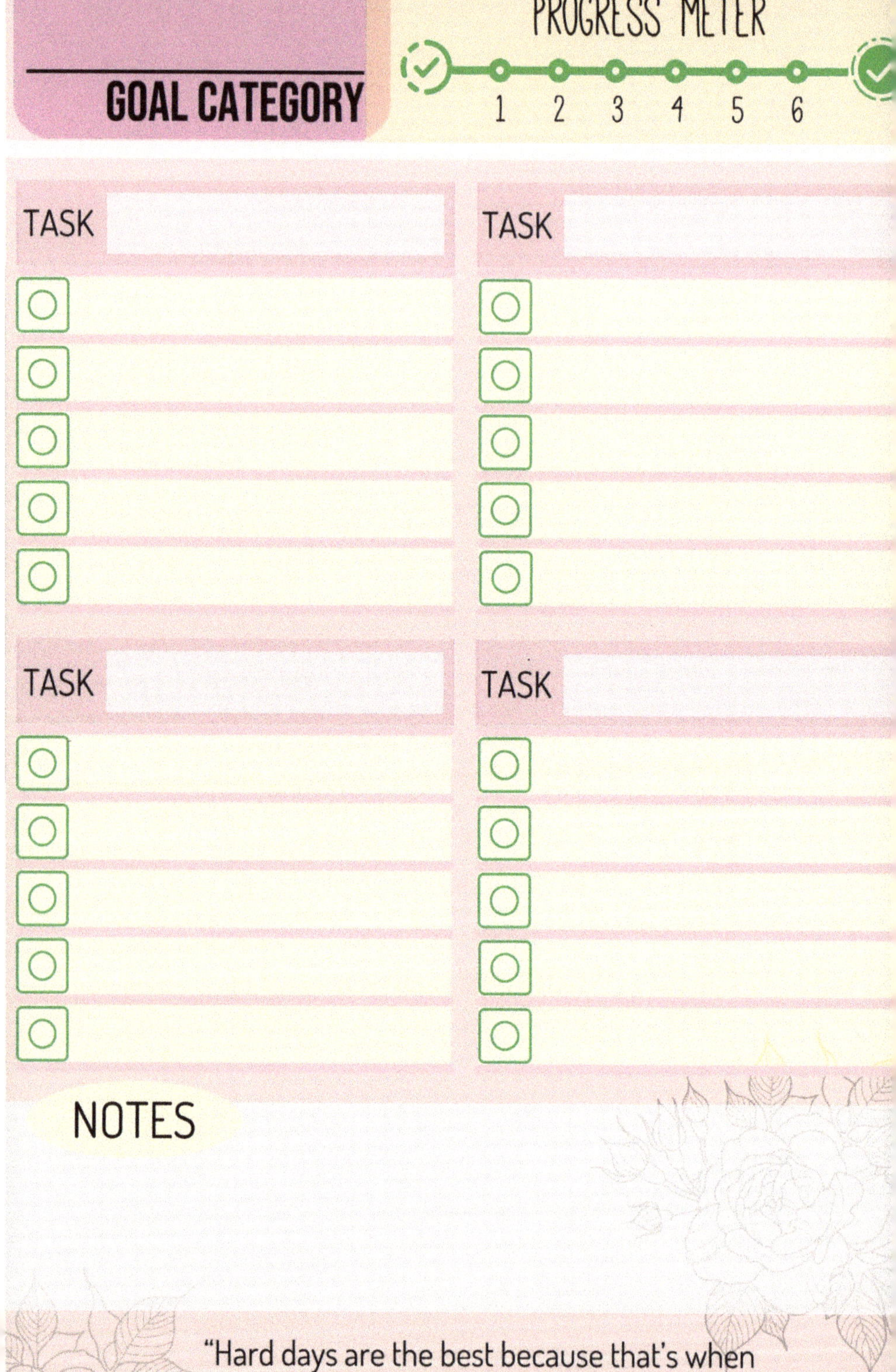

"Hard days are the best because that's when champions are made." -Gabby Douglas

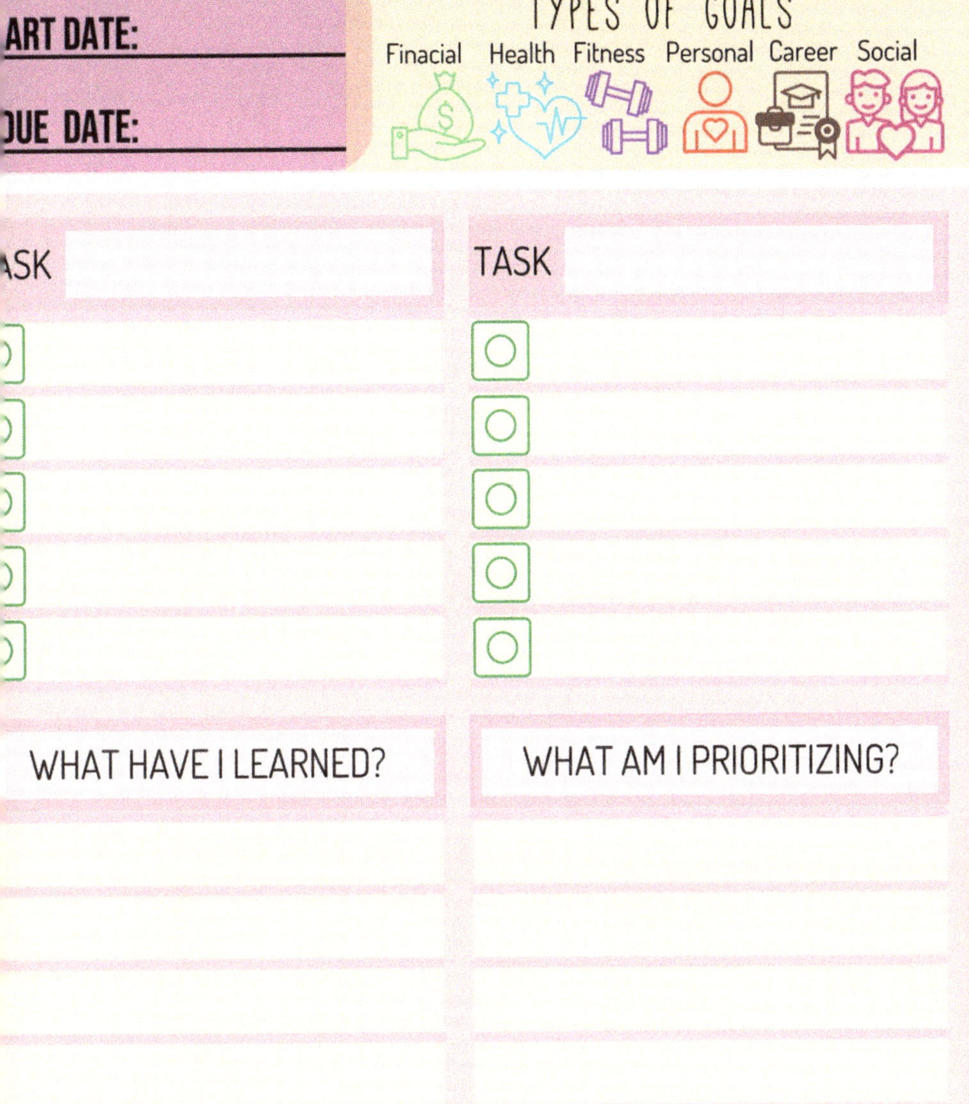

ART DATE:

UE DATE:

TYPES OF GOALS

Finacial Health Fitness Personal Career Social

SK

TASK

WHAT HAVE I LEARNED?

WHAT AM I PRIORITIZING?

NOTES

"Talent is God given. Be humble. Fame is man-given. Be grateful. Conceit is self-given. Be careful." - John Wooden

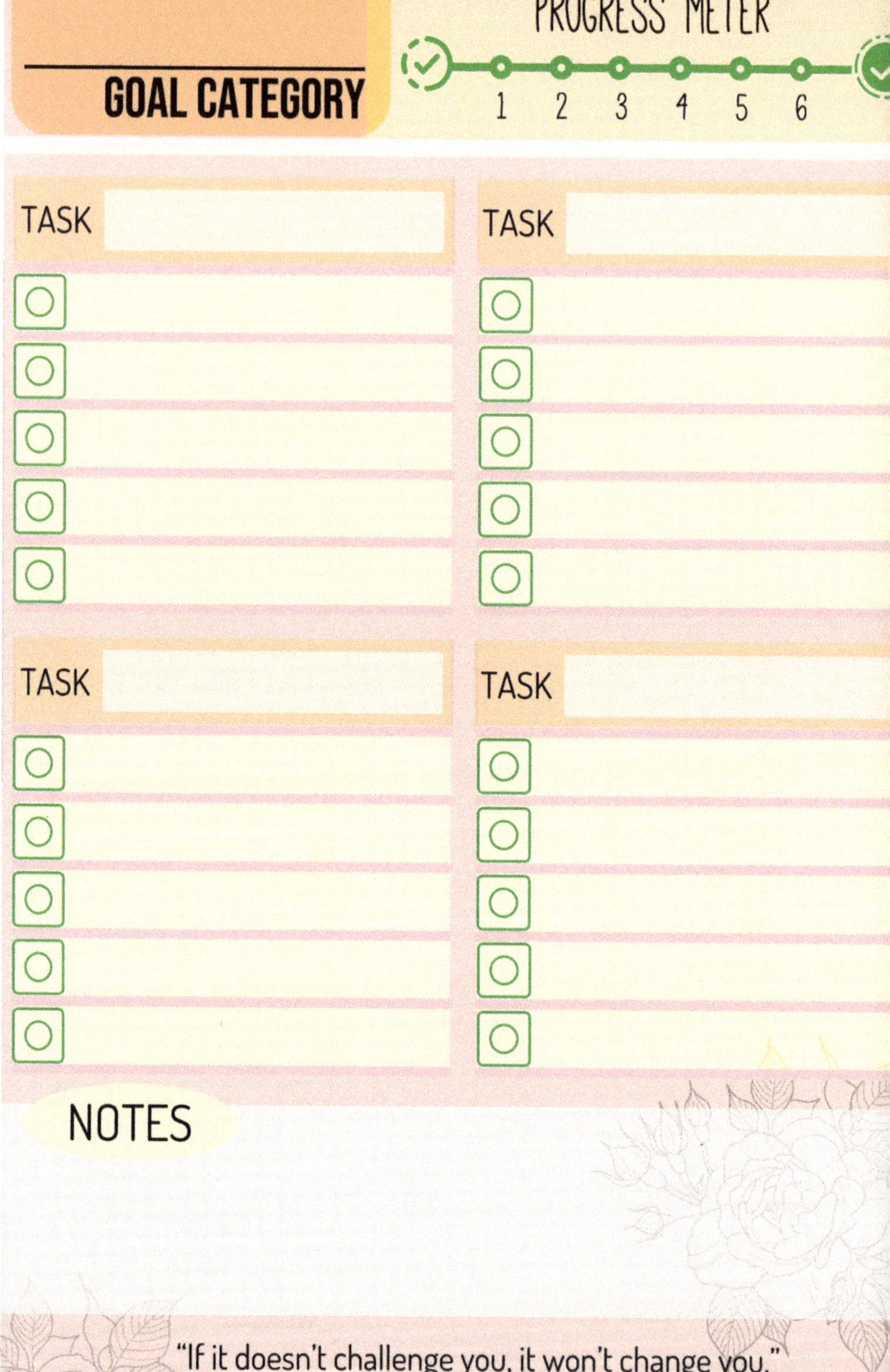

"If it doesn't challenge you, it won't change you."
-Fred Devito

ART DATE: ____________

DUE DATE: ____________

TYPES OF GOALS

Finacial Health Fitness Personal Career Social

ASK

TASK

WHAT HAVE I LEARNED?

WHAT AM I PRIORITIZING?

NOTES

"I think team first. It allows me to succeed, and it allows my team to succeed." -Lebron James

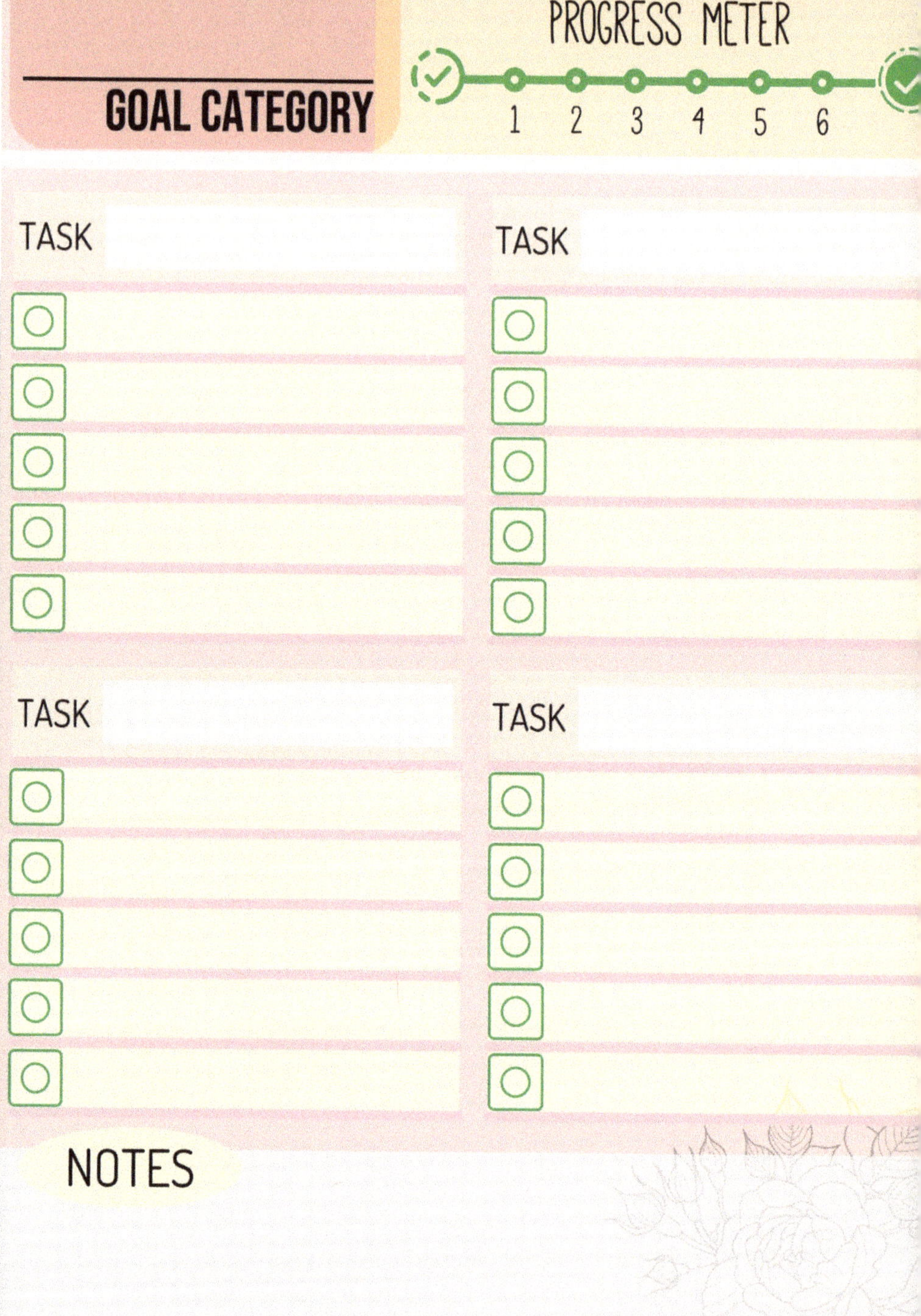

"I may win and I may lose, but I will never be defeated." -Emmitt Smith

ART DATE:

UE DATE:

TYPES OF GOALS

Finacial Health Fitness Personal Career Social

ASK

TASK

WHAT HAVE I LEARNED?

WHAT AM I PRIORITIZING?

NOTES

"If you want to be the best, you have to do the things that other people aren't willing to do." -Michael Phelps

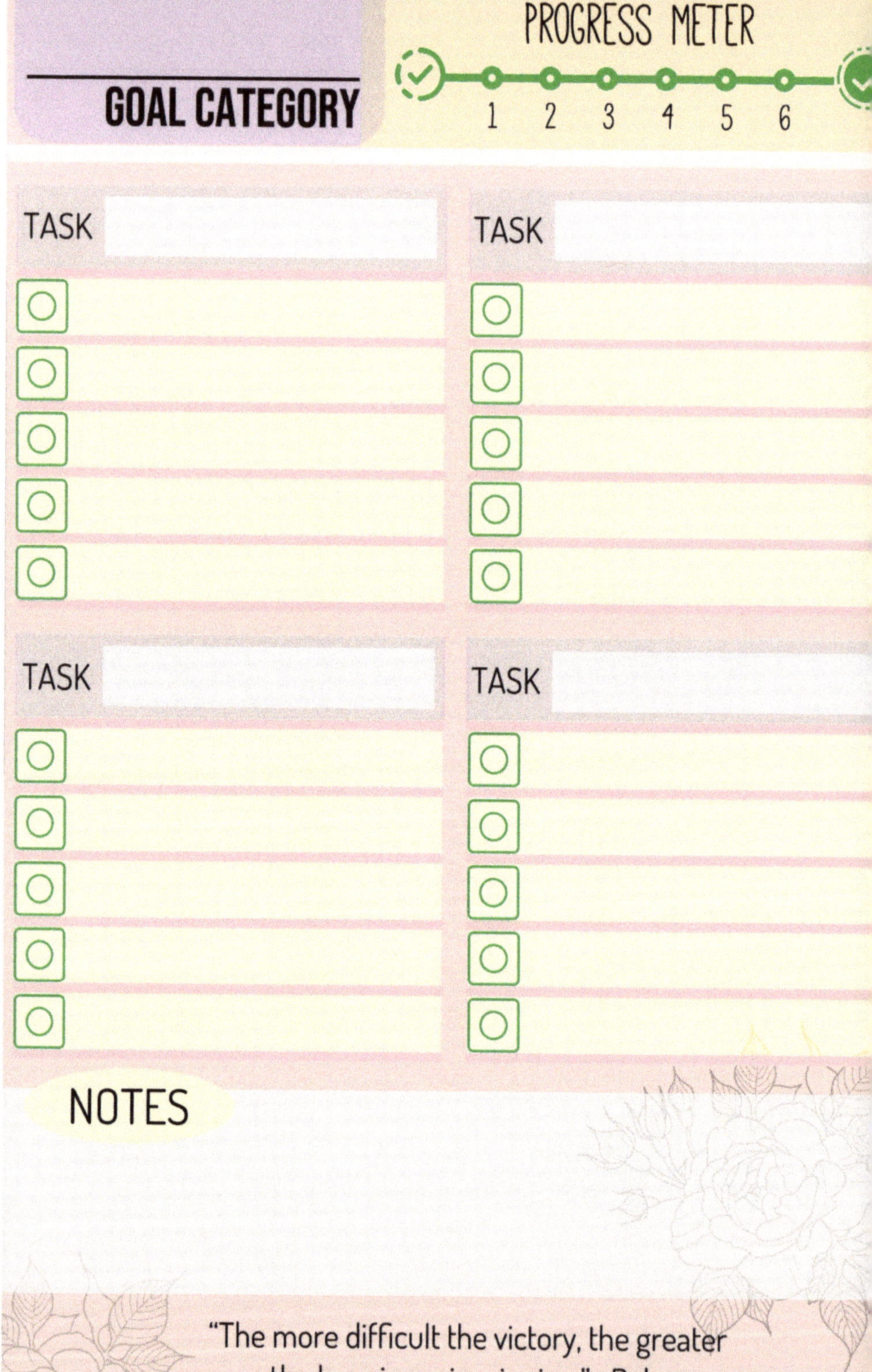

"The more difficult the victory, the greater the happiness in winning." -Pele

TART DATE:

DUE DATE:

TYPES OF GOALS

Finacial Health Fitness Personal Career Social

ASK

TASK

WHAT HAVE I LEARNED?

WHAT AM I PRIORITIZING?

NOTES

"Today I will do what others won't, so tomorrow I can accomplish what others can't" -Jerry Rice

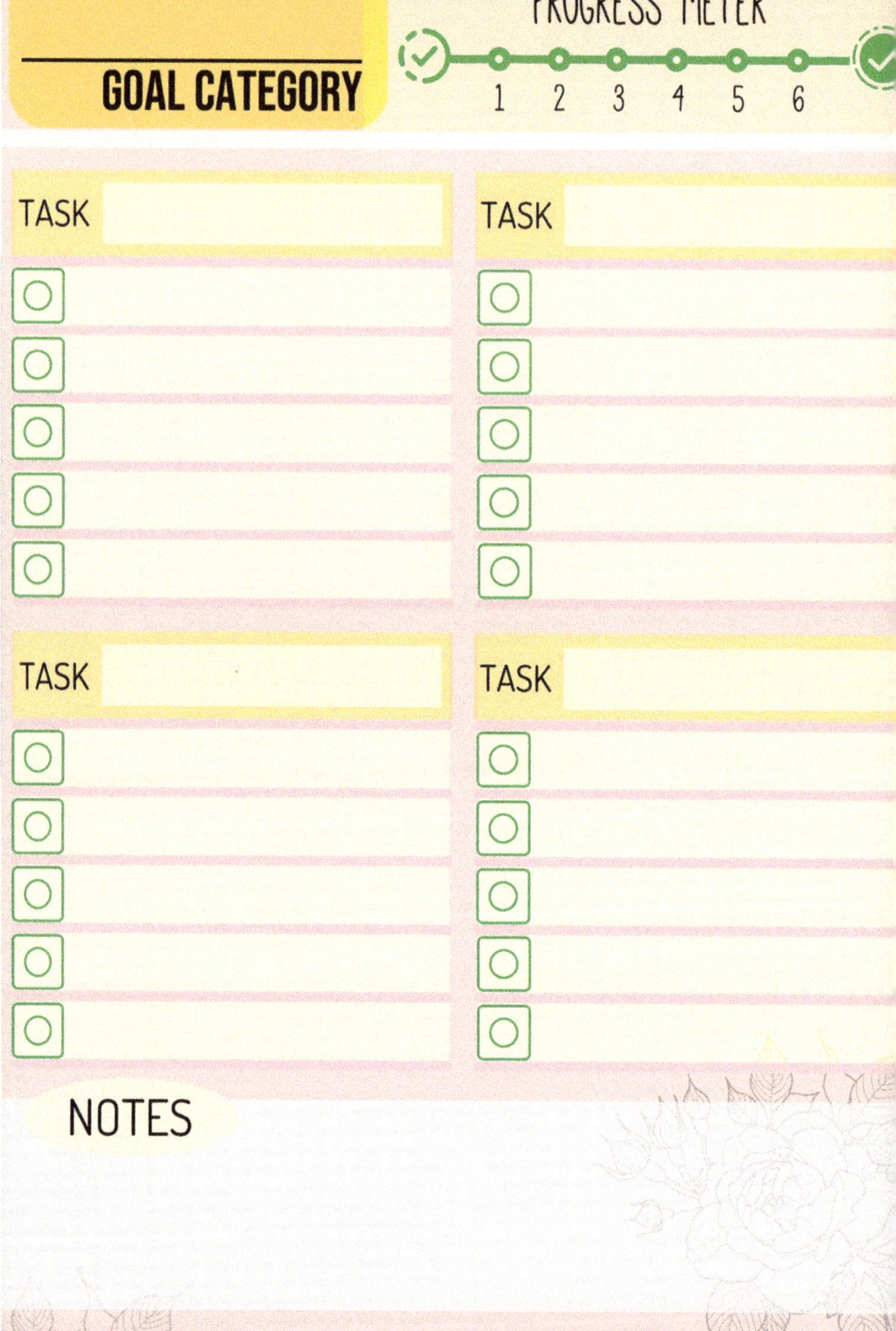

"Every champion was once a contender that refused to give up." -Rocky Balboa

ART DATE:

DUE DATE:

TYPES OF GOALS

Finacial Health Fitness Personal Career Social

ASK

TASK

WHAT HAVE I LEARNED?

WHAT AM I PRIORITIZING?

NOTES

"Courage doesn't mean you don't get afraid. Courage means you don't let fear stop you." -Bethany Hamilton

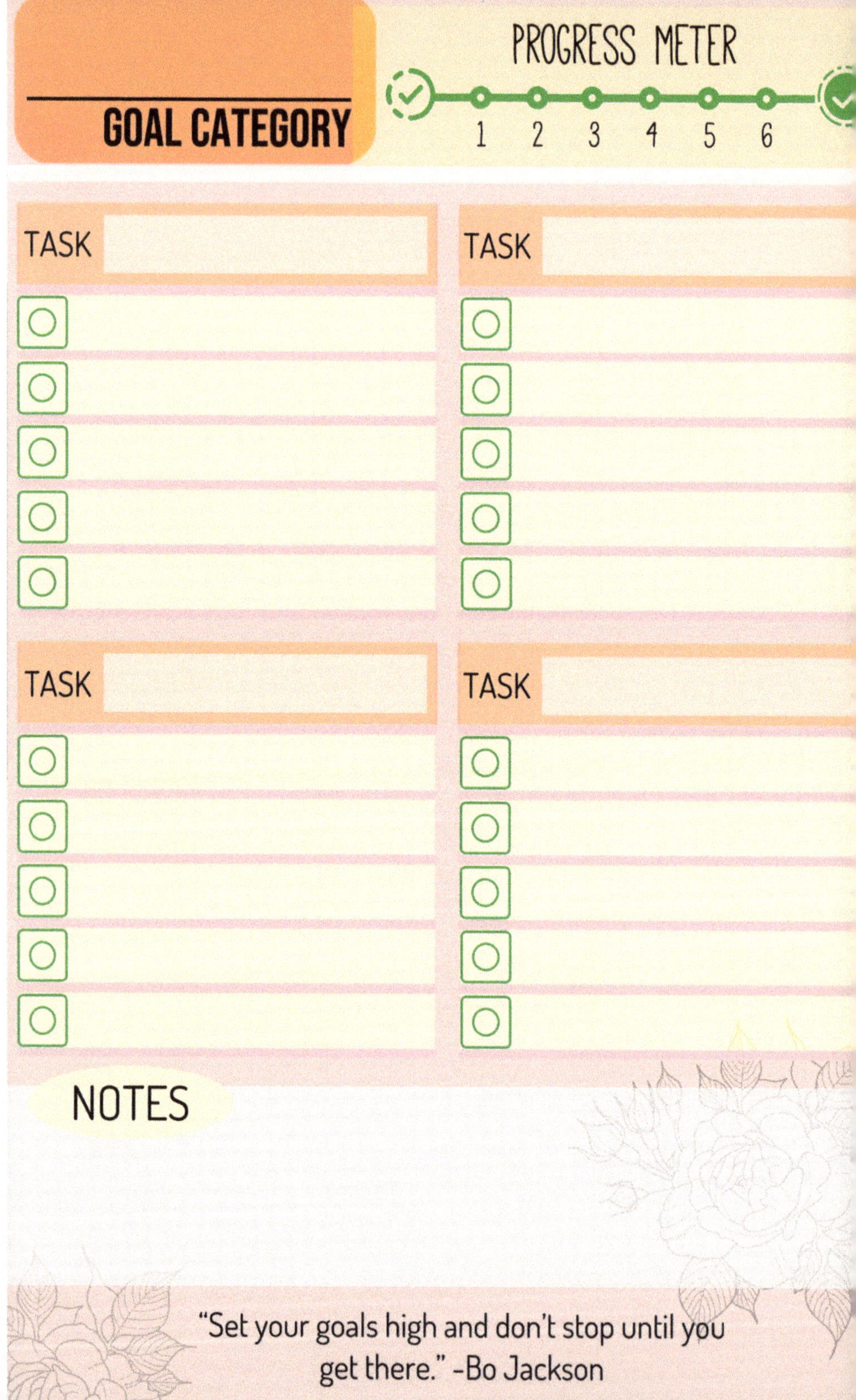
GOAL CATEGORY
PROGRESS METER
1 2 3 4 5 6
TASK
TASK
TASK
TASK
NOTES
"Set your goals high and don't stop until you get there." -Bo Jackson

"Hard work beats talent when talent doesn't work hard." -Tim Notke

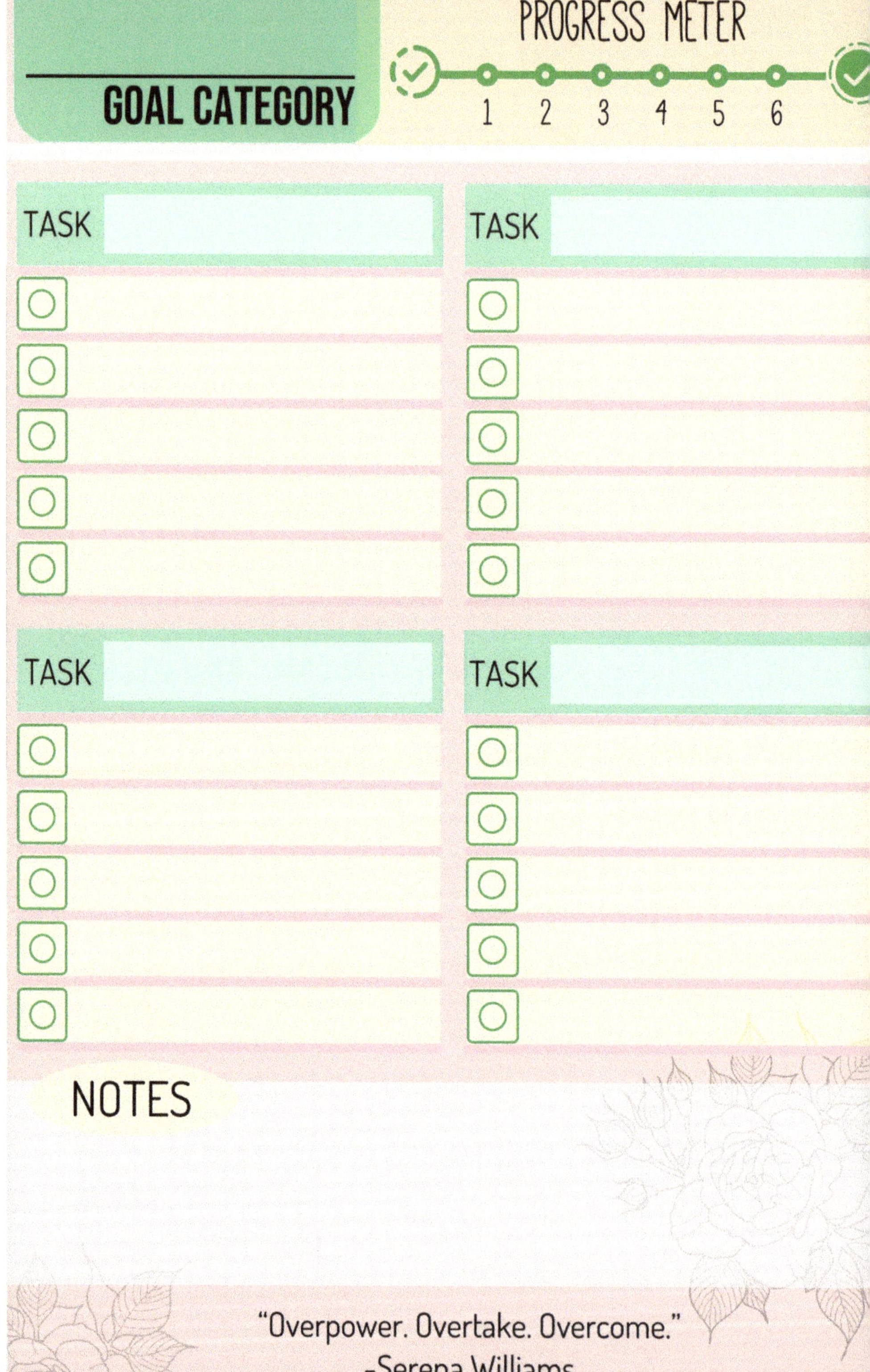
GOAL CATEGORY
PROGRESS METER
1 2 3 4 5 6
TASK
TASK
TASK
TASK
NOTES
"Overpower. Overtake. Overcome."
-Serena Williams

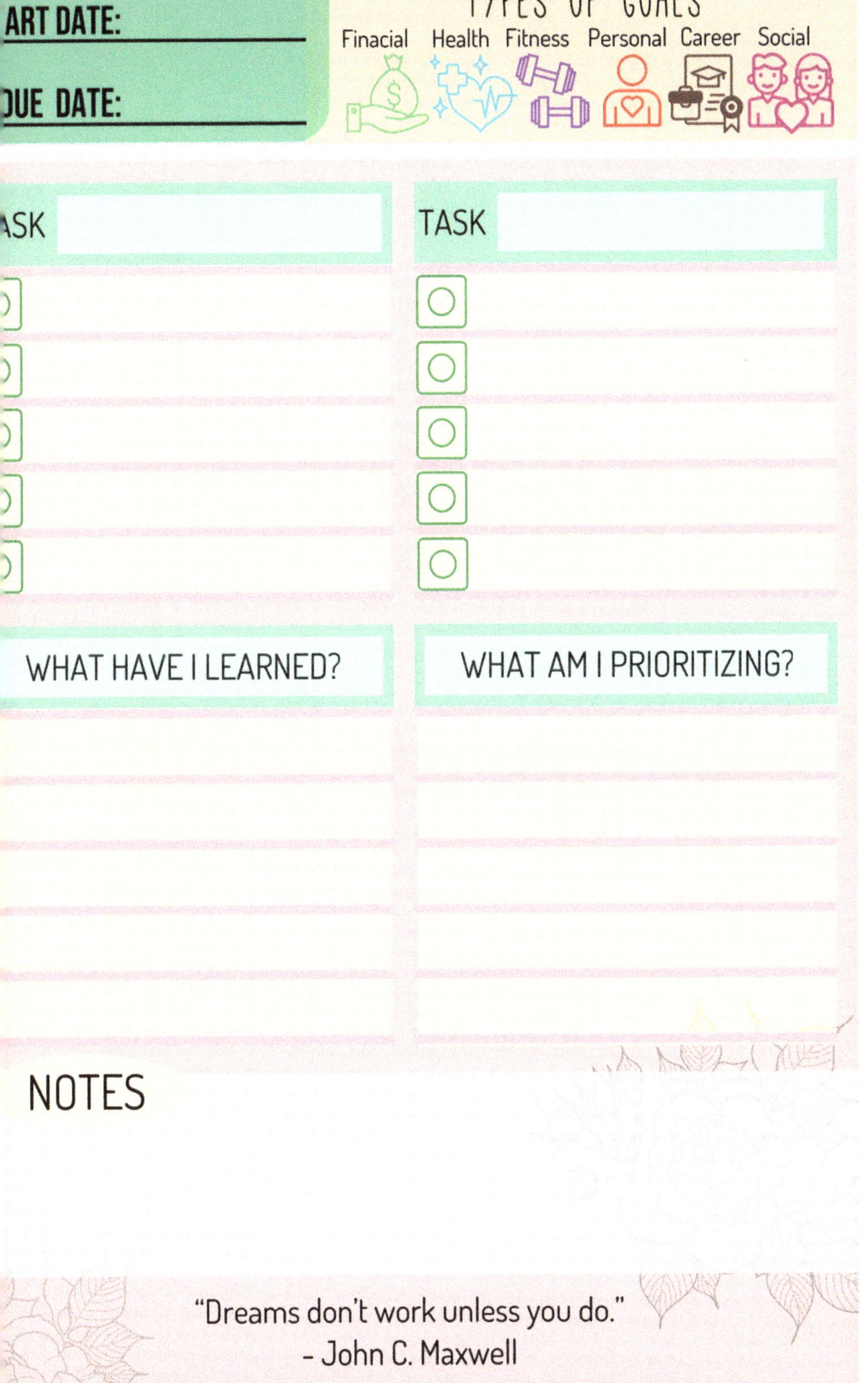
ART DATE:
DUE DATE:
TYPES OF GOALS
Finacial
Health
Fitness
Personal
Career
Social
ASK
TASK
WHAT HAVE I LEARNED?
WHAT AM I PRIORITIZING?
NOTES
“Dreams don’t work unless you do.”
- John C. Maxwell

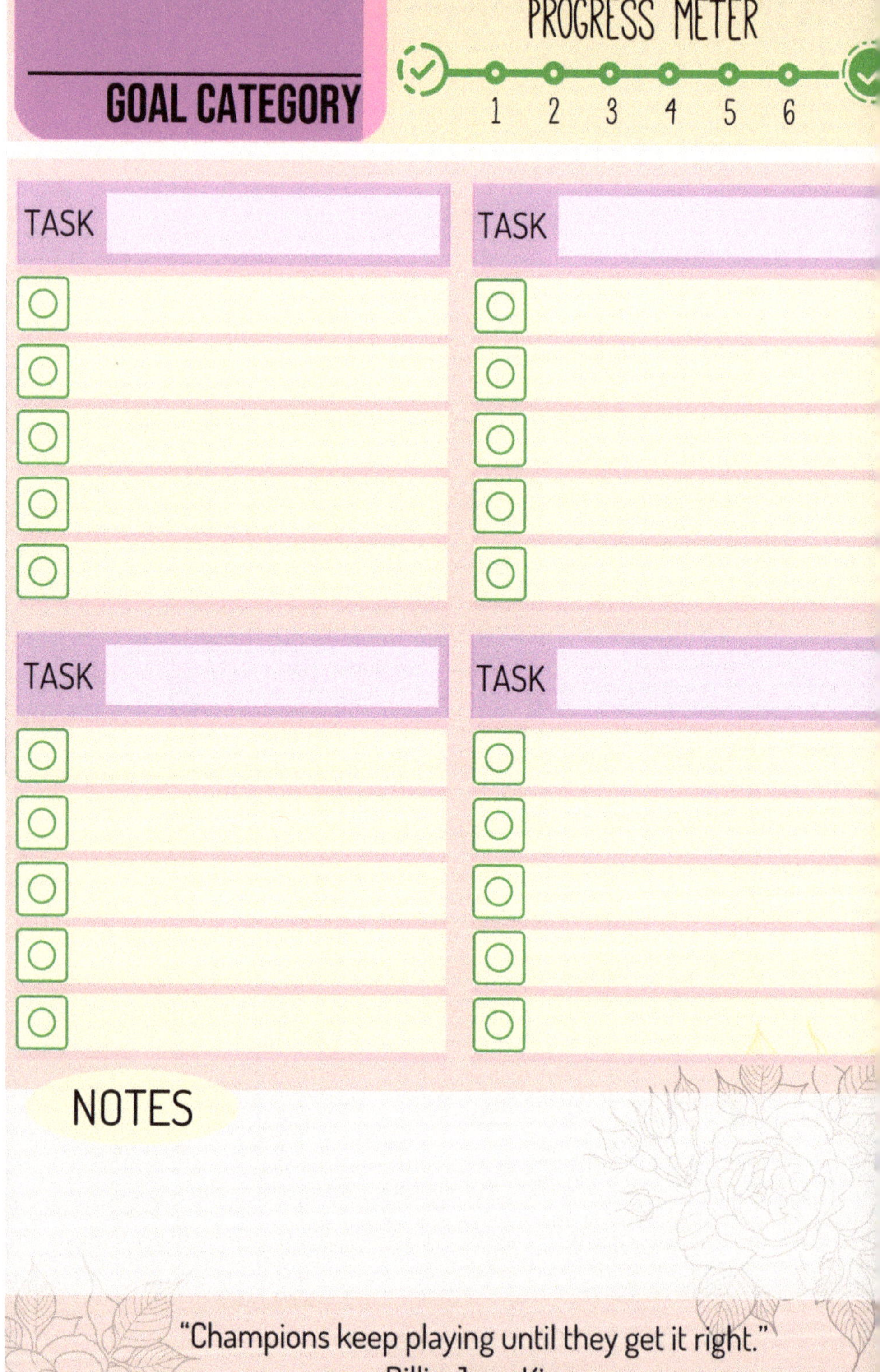

"Champions keep playing until they get it right."
-Billie Jean King

TART DATE:
DUE DATE:
TYPES OF GOALS
Finacial
Health
Fitness
Personal
Career
Social
ASK
TASK
WHAT HAVE I LEARNED?
WHAT AM I PRIORITIZING?
NOTES
"Success is not what you have, but
who you are." -Bo Bennett

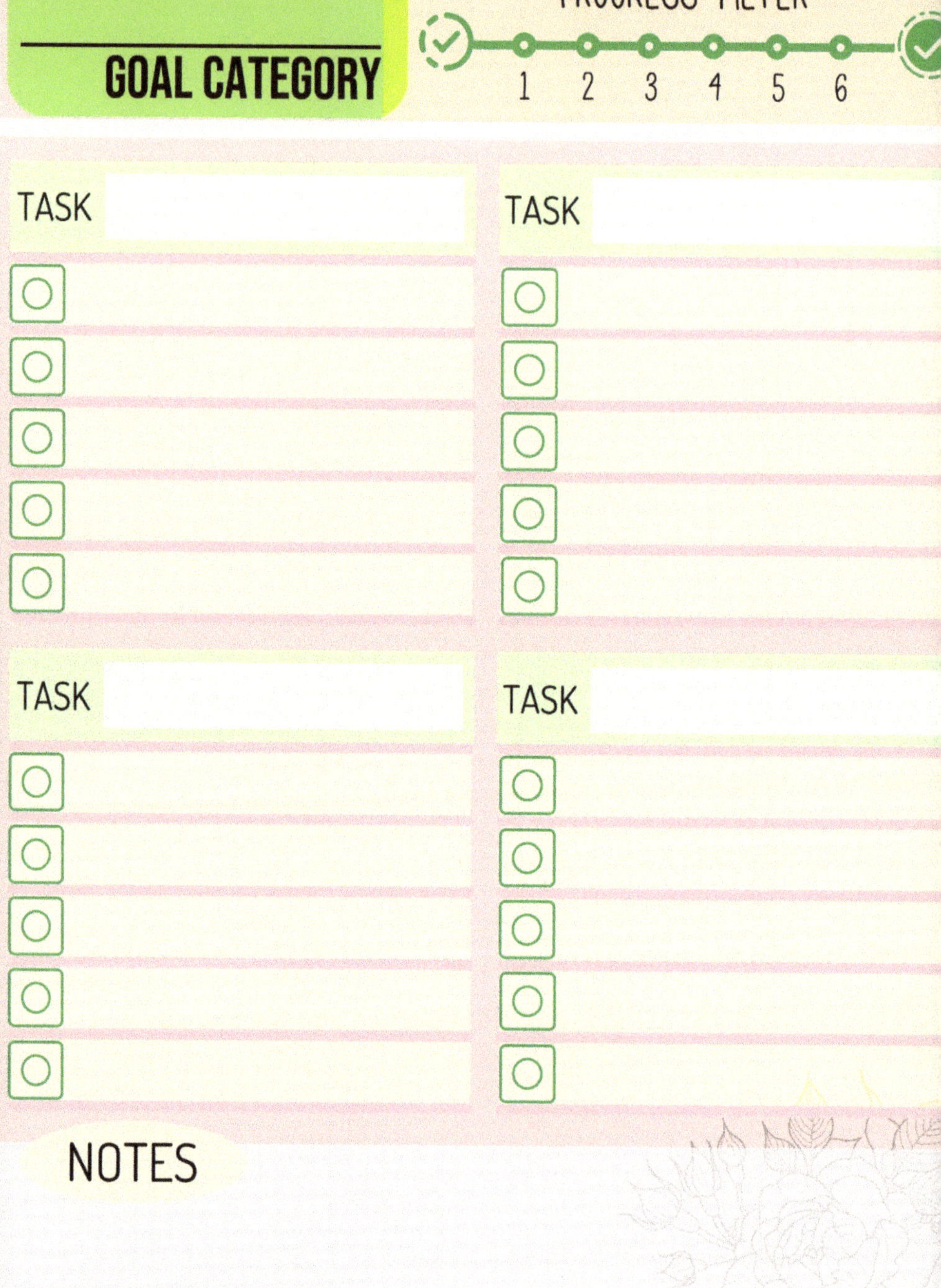

NOTES

"You can't climb the ladder of success with your hands in your pockets." -Arnold Schwarzenegger

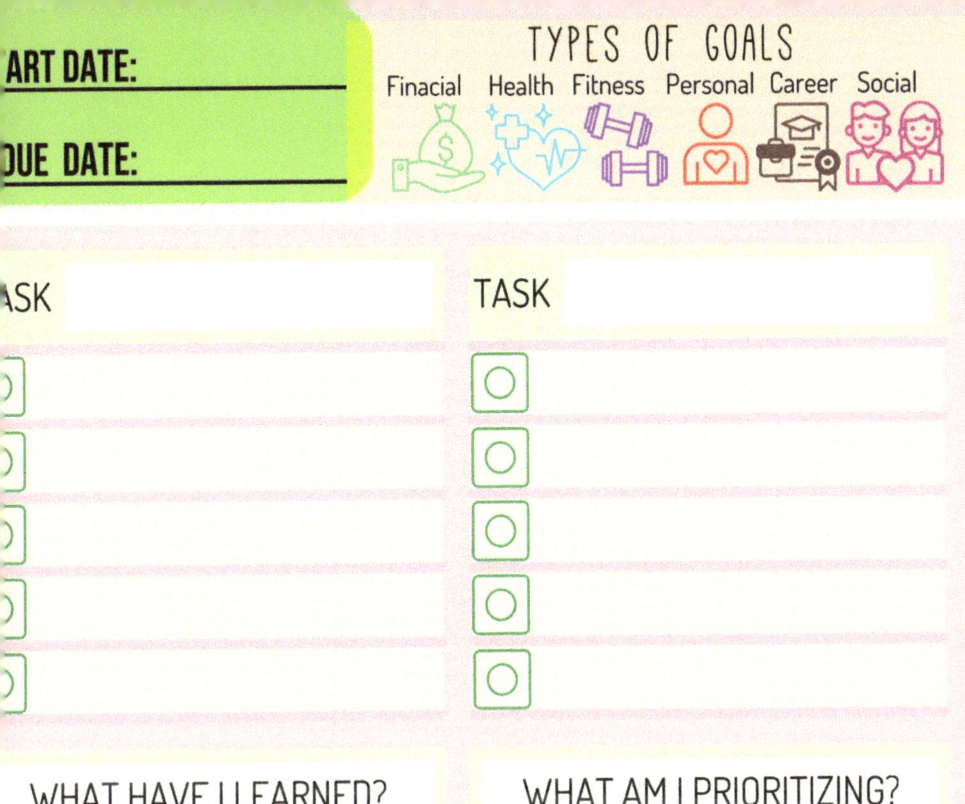

WHAT HAVE I LEARNED?

WHAT AM I PRIORITIZING?

NOTES

"The greatest pleasure of life is doing what people say you cannot do." -Walter Bagehot

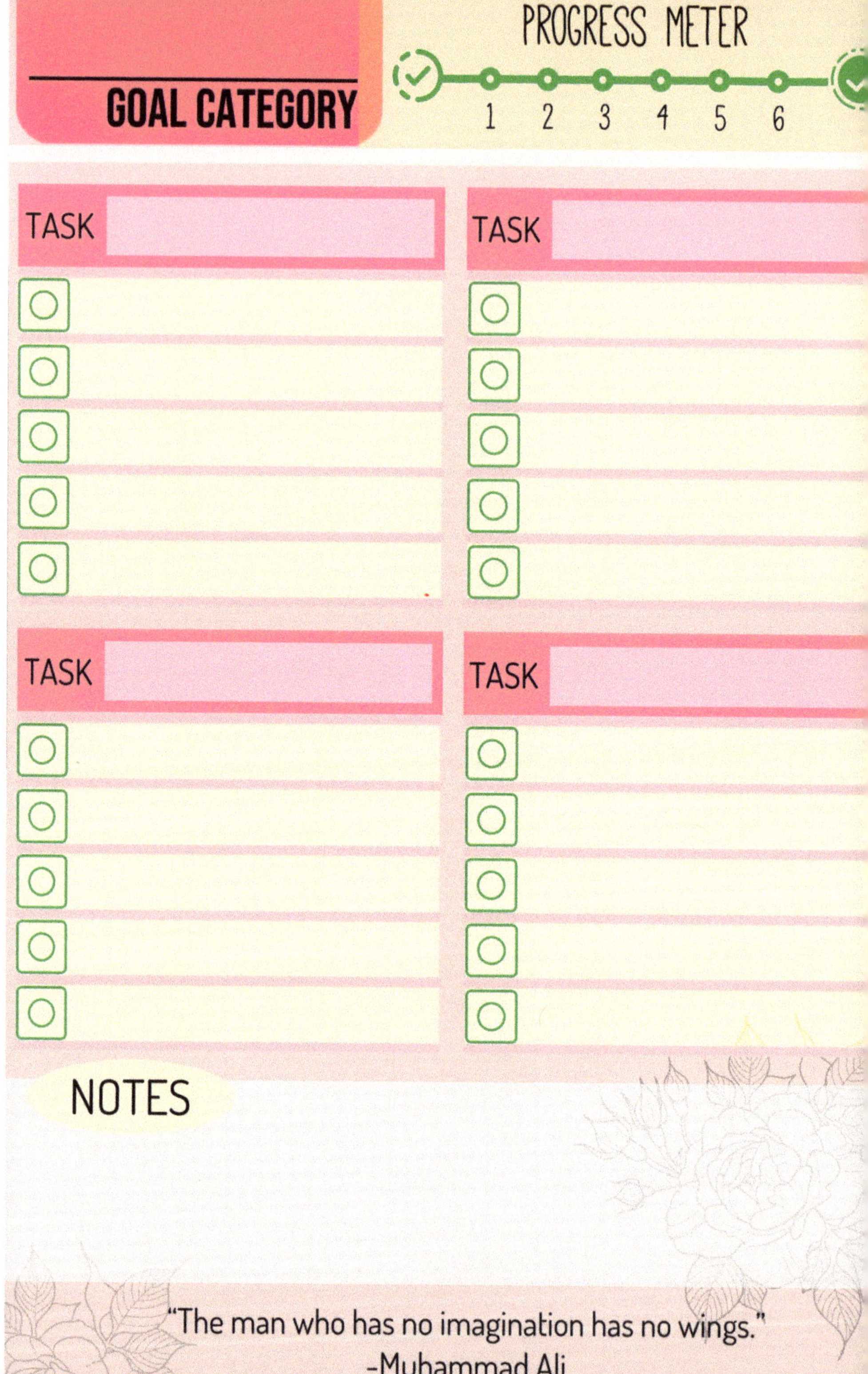
GOAL CATEGORY
PROGRESS METER
1 2 3 4 5 6
TASK
TASK
TASK
TASK
NOTES
"The man who has no imagination has no wings."
-Muhammad Ali

"Age is no barrier. It's a limitation you put on your mind." -Jackie Joyner-Kersee

GOAL MAPPING

GOAL CATEGORIES

- ○
- ○
- ○
- ○
- ○
- ○
- ○
- ○
- ○
- ○
- ○
- ○
- ○
- ○
- ○

WHICH HABITS SHOULD I MAINTAIN TO COMPLETE MY GOALS?

HOW SHOULD I PLAN MY DAILY ROUTINE TO COMPLETE MY GOALS?

NOTES

"Once you learn to quit, it becomes a habit."

-Vince Lombardi

PLANNER

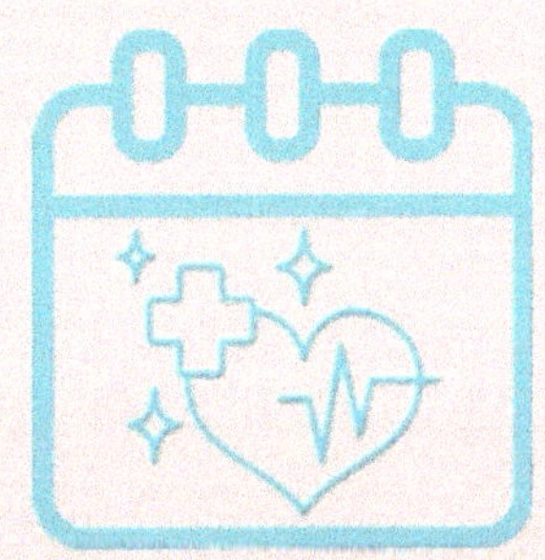

GROW 2025 THRIVE

PLAN YOUR GOALS

2025

THERE IS ALWAYS AN OPPORTUNITY TO START NEW

JANUARY

SUN	MON	TUE	WED	THU	FRI	SAT
29	30	31	01 New Year's Day	02	03	04
05	06	07	08	09	10	11
12	13	14	15	16	17	18
19	20 Martin Luther King Jr. Day	21	22	23	24	25
26	27	28	29 Lunar New Year	30	31	01
02	03					

REMINDERS:

JANUARY GOALS

HIS MONTH I WANT TO ACCOMPLISH:

HIS MONTH'S GOAL CATEGORY FOCUS:

1

2

3

4

5

6

HOW CAN I IMPROVE:

HABITS TO ESTABLISH:

2025 JANUARY

I AM...

POSITIVE AFFIRMATIONS

January						
Su	Mo	Tu	We	Th	Fr	Sa
			1	2	3	4
5	6	7	8	9	10	11
12	13	14	15	16	17	18
19	20	21	22	23	24	25
26	27	28	29	30	31	

30 MONDAY

31 TUESDAY New Year's Eve

01 WEDNESDAY New Year's Day

02 THURSDAY

GOALS TO COMPLETE

03 FRIDAY

04 SATURDAY

05 SUNDAY

NOTES

"Don't give up on your dreams, or your dreams will give up on you." -John Wooden

2025 JANUARY

I AM...

POSITIVE AFFIRMATIONS

January					
Su	Mo	Tu	We	Th	Fr
			1	2	3
5	6	7	8	9	10
12	13	14	15	16	17
19	20	21	22	23	24
26	27	28	29	30	31

06 MONDAY

07 TUESDAY

08 WEDNESDAY

09 THURSDAY

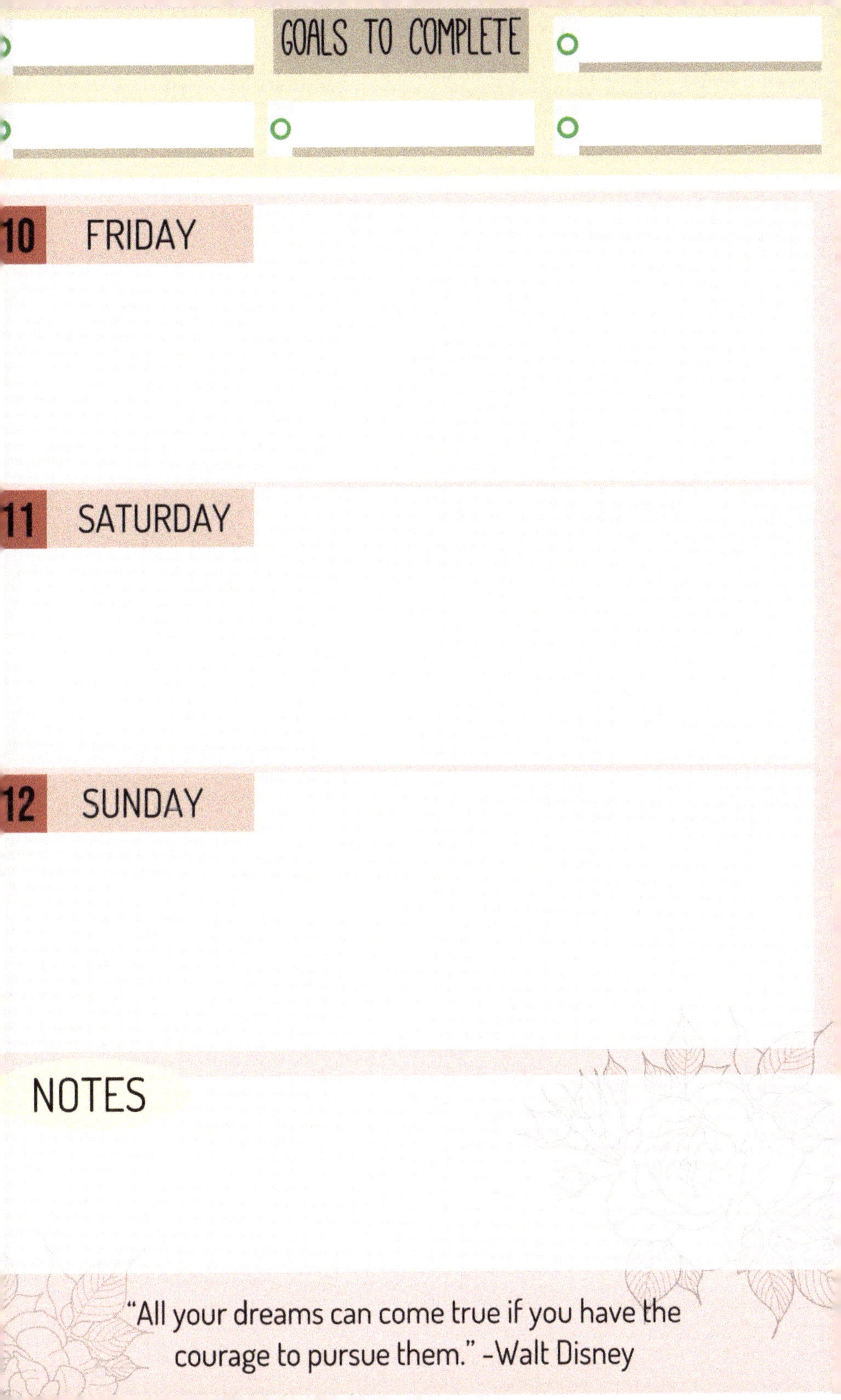
GOALS TO COMPLETE
10 FRIDAY
11 SATURDAY
12 SUNDAY
NOTES
"All your dreams can come true if you have the courage to pursue them." -Walt Disney

2025
JANUARY

I AM...

POSITIVE AFFIRMATIONS

January						
Su	Mo	Tu	We	Th	Fr	Sa
			1	2	3	4
5	6	7	8	9	10	11
12	13	14	15	16	17	18
19	20	21	22	23	24	25
26	27	28	29	30	31	

13 MONDAY

14 TUESDAY

15 WEDNESDAY

16 THURSDAY

GOALS TO COMPLETE

17 FRIDAY

18 SATURDAY

19 SUNDAY

NOTES

"When something is important enough, you do it even if the odds are not in your favor." -Elon Musk

2025
JANUARY

I AM...

POSITIVE AFFIRMATIONS

January						
Su	Mo	Tu	We	Th	Fr	S
			1	2	3	4
5	6	7	8	9	10	1
12	13	14	15	16	17	1
19	20	21	22	23	24	2
26	27	28	29	30	31	

20 MONDAY

Martin Luther King Jr. Day

21 TUESDAY

22 WEDNESDAY

23 THURSDAY

GOALS TO COMPLETE

24 FRIDAY

25 SATURDAY

26 SUNDAY

NOTES

"If you find it in your heart to care for somebody else,
you will have succeeded." -Maya Angelou

2025 JANUARY

I AM...

POSITIVE AFFIRMATIONS

January						
Su	Mo	Tu	We	Th	Fr	Sa
			1	2	3	4
5	6	7	8	9	10	11
12	13	14	15	16	17	18
19	20	21	22	23	24	25
26	27	28	29	30	31	

27 MONDAY

28 TUESDAY

29 WEDNESDAY Lunar New Year

30 THURSDAY

GOALS TO COMPLETE

31 FRIDAY

01 SATURDAY

02 SUNDAY

Ground Hog's Day

NOTES

"Success is failing nine times and getting up ten."
-Jon Bon Jovi

2025

KEEP MAKING PROGRESS NO MATTER HOW SMALL THE STEP

FEBRUARY

SUN	MON	TUE	WED	THU	FRI	SAT
26	27	28	29	30	31	01
02 Ground Hog's Day	03	04	05	06	07	08
09	10	11	12	13	14 Valentine's Day	15
16	17 President's Day	18	19	20	21	22
23	24	25	26	27	28	01
02	03					

REMINDERS:

FEBRUARY GOALS

HIS MONTH I WANT TO ACCOMPLISH:

HIS MONTH'S GOAL CATEGORY FOCUS:

1

2

3

4

5

6

HOW CAN I IMPROVE:

HABITS TO ESTABLISH:

2025 FEBRUARY

I AM...

POSITIVE AFFIRMATIONS

February						
Su	Mo	Tu	We	Th	Fr	Sa
						1
2	3	4	5	6	7	8
9	10	11	12	13	14	15
16	17	18	19	20	21	22
23	24	25	26	27	28	

03 MONDAY

04 TUESDAY

05 WEDNESDAY

06 THURSDAY

GOALS TO COMPLETE
07 FRIDAY
08 SATURDAY
09 SUNDAY
NOTES
“There is no success without hardship.”
-Sophocles

2025 FEBRUARY

I AM...

POSITIVE AFFIRMATIONS

February					
Su	Mo	Tu	We	Th	Fr
2	3	4	5	6	7
9	10	11	12	13	14
16	17	18	19	20	21
23	24	25	26	27	28

10 MONDAY

11 TUESDAY

12 WEDNESDAY

13 THURSDAY

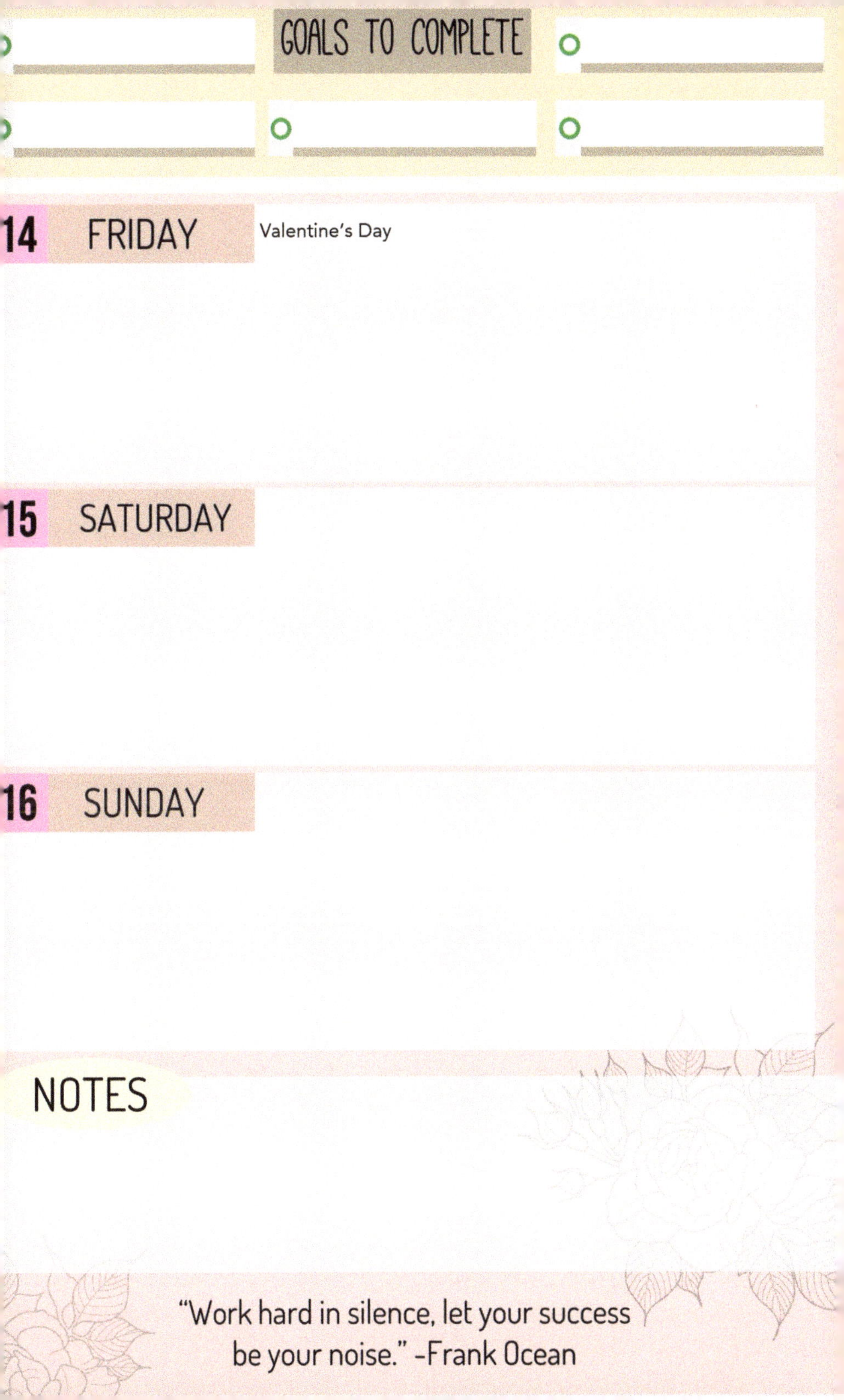

GOALS TO COMPLETE

- ○
- ○
- ○
- ○
- ○

14 FRIDAY

Valentine's Day

15 SATURDAY

16 SUNDAY

NOTES

"Work hard in silence, let your success be your noise." -Frank Ocean

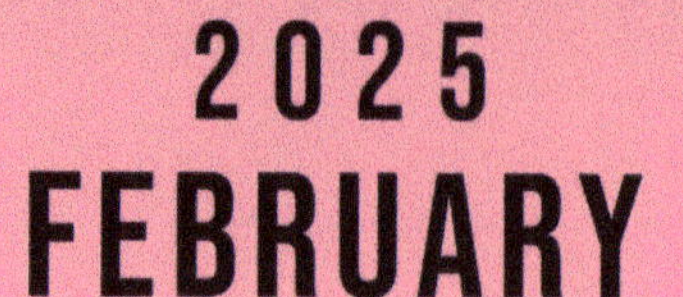

I AM...

POSITIVE AFFIRMATIONS

February

Su	Mo	Tu	We	Th	Fr	Sa
						1
2	3	4	5	6	7	8
9	10	11	12	13	14	15
16	17	18	19	20	21	22
23	24	25	26	27	28	

17 MONDAY

President's Day

18 TUESDAY

19 WEDNESDAY

20 THURSDAY

GOALS TO COMPLETE

21 FRIDAY

22 SATURDAY

23 SUNDAY

NOTES

“Great achievement is usually born of great sacrifice, and is never the result of selfishness.” -Napoleon Hill

2025 FEBRUARY

I AM...

POSITIVE AFFIRMATIONS

February					
Su	Mo	Tu	We	Th	Fr
2	3	4	5	6	7
9	10	11	12	13	14
16	17	18	19	20	21
23	24	25	26	27	28

24 MONDAY

25 TUESDAY

26 WEDNESDAY

27 THURSDAY

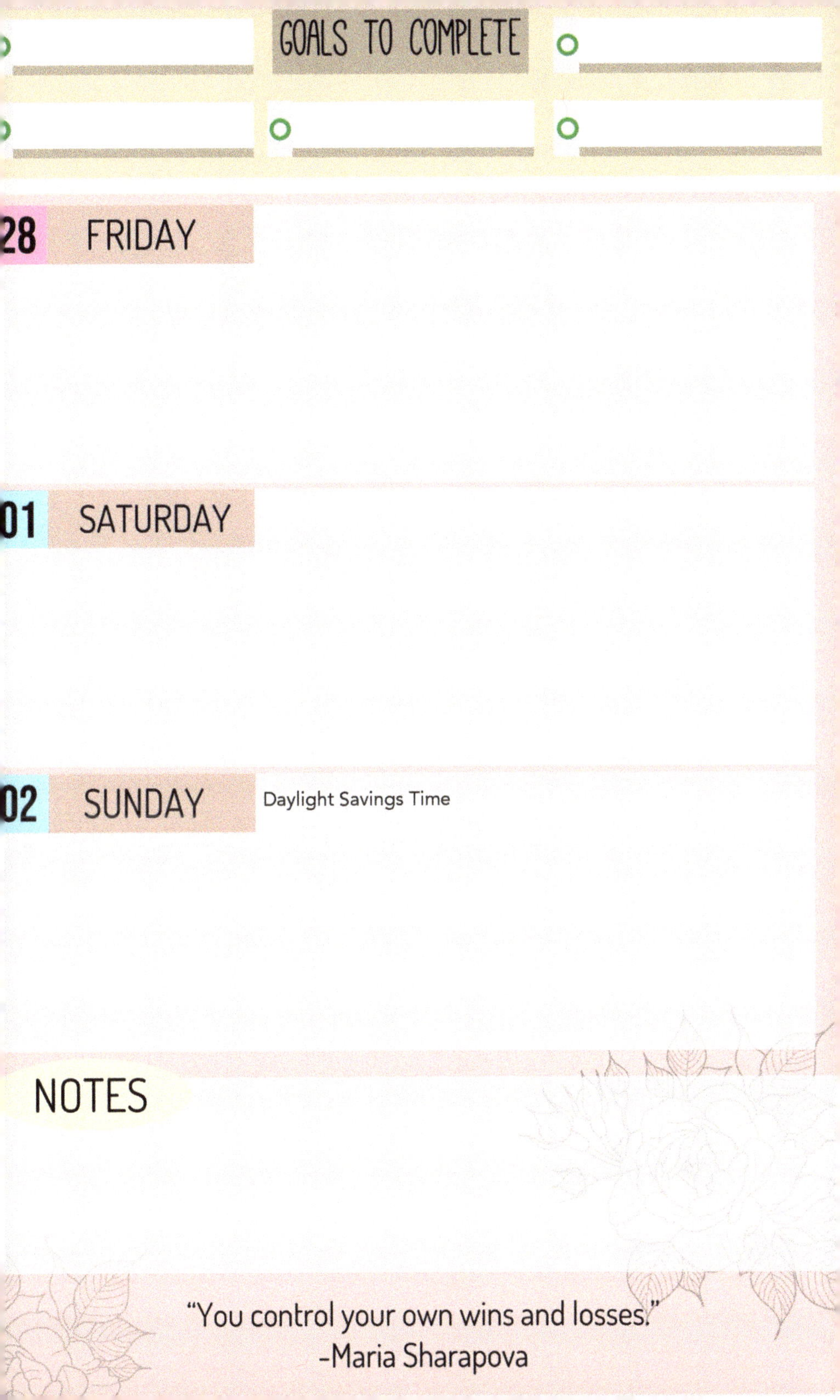

GOALS TO COMPLETE

28 FRIDAY

01 SATURDAY

02 SUNDAY

Daylight Savings Time

NOTES

"You control your own wins and losses."
-Maria Sharapova

2025

YOU ARE WORTH IT!
KEEP GOING!

MARCH

SUN	MON	TUE	WED	THU	FRI	SAT
23	24	25	26	27	27	01
02 Daylight Savings Time	03	04	05 Ash Wednesday	06	07	08
09	10	11	12	13	14	15
16	17 St. Patrick's Day	18	19	20	21	22
23	24	25	26	27	28	29
30	31					

REMINDERS:

MARCH GOALS

HIS MONTH I WANT TO ACCOMPLISH:

HIS MONTH'S GOAL CATEGORY FOCUS:

1

2

3

4

5

6

HOW CAN I IMPROVE:

HABITS TO ESTABLISH:

2025
MARCH

I AM...

POSITIVE AFFIRMATIONS

March					
Su	Mo	Tu	We	Th	Fr
2	3	4	5	6	7
9	10	11	12	13	14
16	17	18	19	20	21
23	24	25	26	27	28
30	31				

03 MONDAY

04 TUESDAY

05 WEDNESDAY

Ash Wednesday

06 THURSDAY

GOALS TO COMPLETE

07 FRIDAY

08 SATURDAY

09 SUNDAY

NOTES

“If you set your goals ridiculously high and it's a failure, you will fail above everyone else's success.” –James Cameron

I AM...

POSITIVE AFFIRMATIONS

March						
Su	Mo	Tu	We	Th	Fr	Sa
						1
2	3	4	5	6	7	8
9	10	11	12	13	14	
16	17	18	19	20	21	
23	24	25	26	27	28	
30	31					

10 MONDAY

11 TUESDAY

12 WEDNESDAY

13 THURSDAY

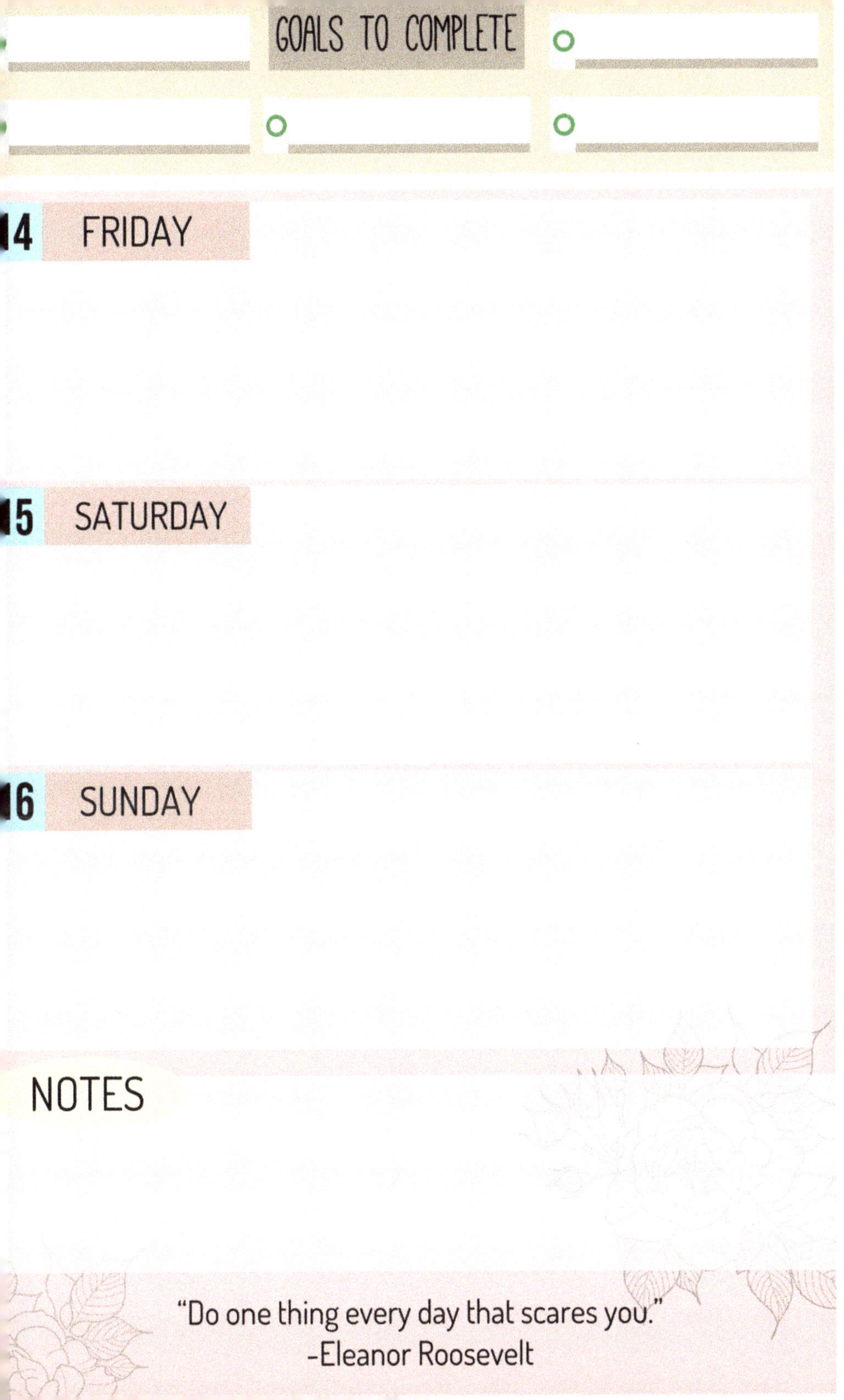

GOALS TO COMPLETE

14 FRIDAY

15 SATURDAY

16 SUNDAY

NOTES

“Do one thing every day that scares you.”
-Eleanor Roosevelt

2025 MARCH

I AM... POSITIVE AFFIRMATIONS

March

Su	Mo	Tu	We	Th	Fr
2	3	4	5	6	7
9	10	11	12	13	14
16	17	18	19	20	21
23	24	25	26	27	28
30	31				

17 MONDAY

St. Patrick's Day

18 TUESDAY

19 WEDNESDAY

20 THURSDAY

GOALS TO COMPLETE

21 FRIDAY

22 SATURDAY

23 SUNDAY

NOTES

"In the end, it's not the years in your life that count. It's the life in your years." -Abraham Lincoln

2025 MARCH

I AM...

POSITIVE AFFIRMATIONS

Su	Mo	Tu	We	Th	Fr	Sa
						1
2	3	4	5	6	7	8
9	10	11	12	13	14	15
16	17	18	19	20	21	22
23	24	25	26	27	28	29
30	31					

March

24 MONDAY

25 TUESDAY

26 WEDNESDAY

27 THURSDAY

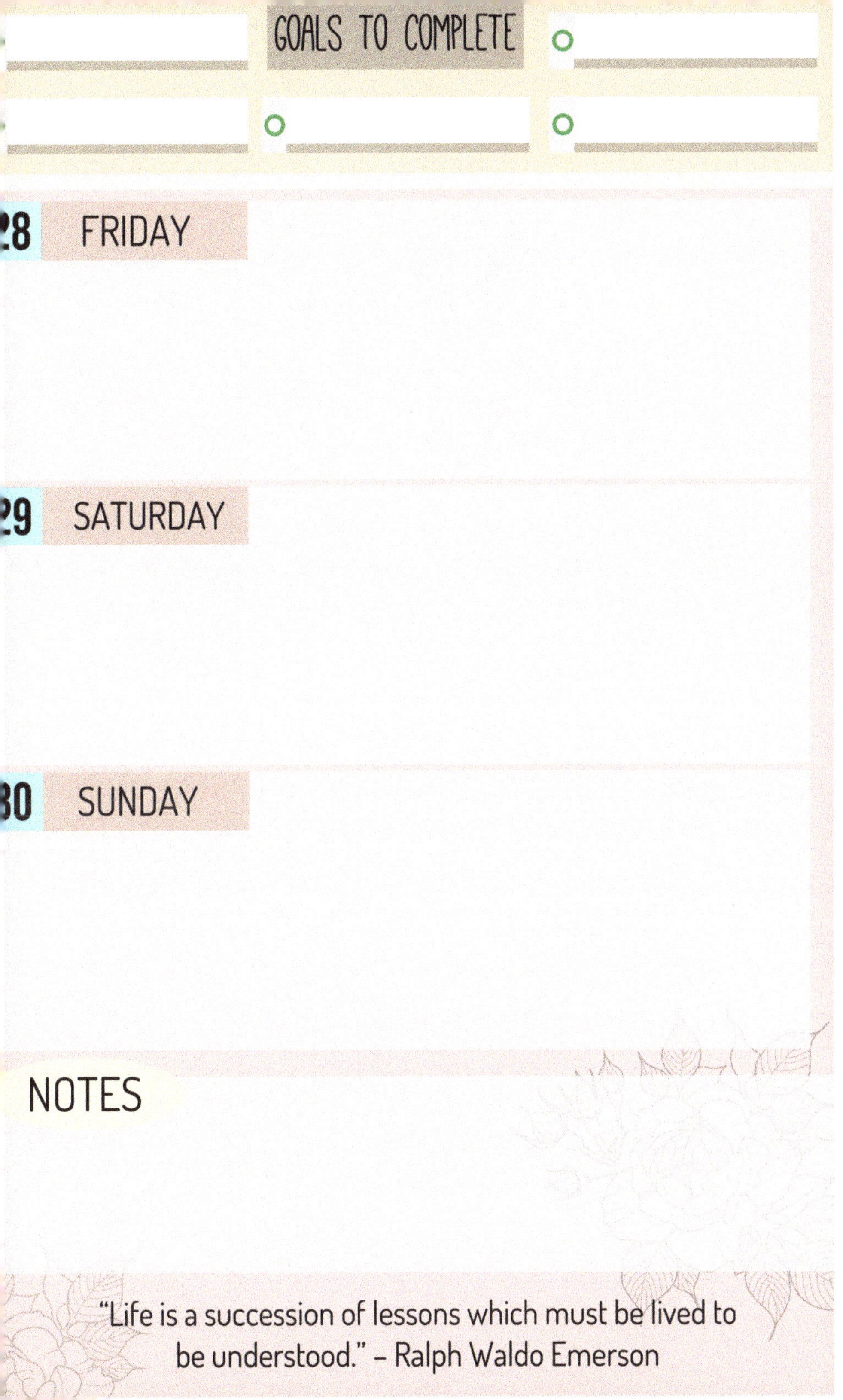

GOALS TO COMPLETE

28 FRIDAY

29 SATURDAY

30 SUNDAY

NOTES

“Life is a succession of lessons which must be lived to be understood.” – Ralph Waldo Emerson

2025

THERE'S MORE TO COME!
HAVE A GOOD ATTITUDE

APRIL

SUN	MON	TUE	WED	THU	FRI	SAT
30	31	01 April Fools' Day	02	03	04	05
06	07	08	09	10	11	12
13 Palm Sunday	14	15	16	17	18 Good Friday	19
20 Easter	21	22 Earth Day	23	24	25	26
27	28	29	30	01	02	03
04	05					

REMINDERS:

APRIL GOALS

HIS MONTH I WANT TO ACCOMPLISH:

HIS MONTH'S GOAL CATEGORY FOCUS:

1

2

3

4

5

6

HOW CAN I IMPROVE:

HABITS TO ESTABLISH:

2025 APRIL

I AM...

POSITIVE AFFIRMATIONS

April

Su	Mo	Tu	We	Th	Fr	Sa
		1	2	3	4	5
6	7	8	9	10	11	12
13	14	15	16	17	18	19
20	21	22	23	24	25	26
27	28	29	30			

31 MONDAY

01 TUESDAY

April Fools' Day

02 WEDNESDAY

03 THURSDAY

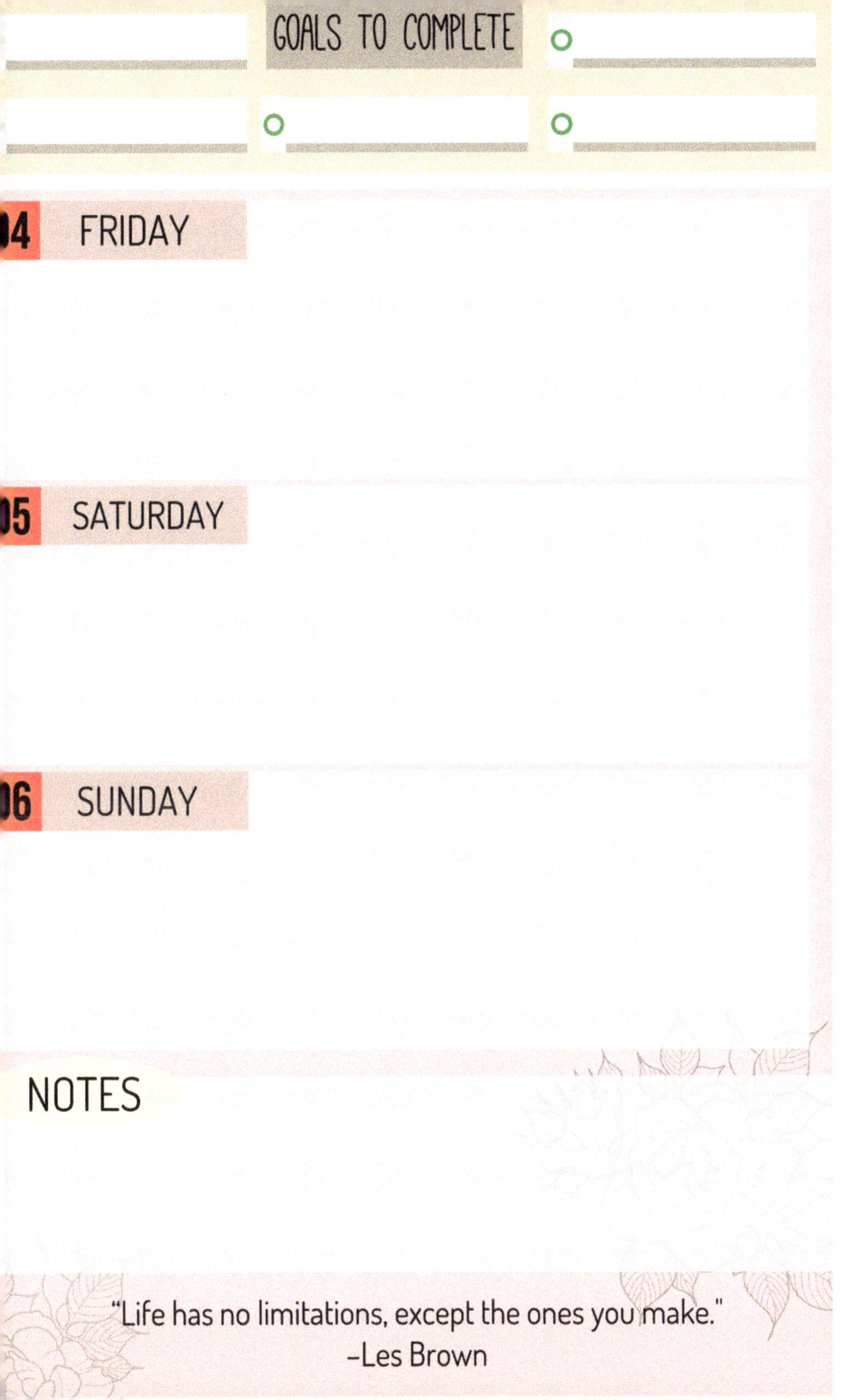
GOALS TO COMPLETE
04 FRIDAY
05 SATURDAY
06 SUNDAY
NOTES
"Life has no limitations, except the ones you make."
–Les Brown

2025 APRIL

I AM...

POSITIVE AFFIRMATIONS

April					
Su	Mo	Tu	We	Th	Fr
		1	2	3	4
6	7	8	9	10	11
13	14	15	16	17	18
20	21	22	23	24	25
27	28	29	30		

07 MONDAY

08 TUESDAY

09 WEDNESDAY

10 THURSDAY

GOALS TO COMPLETE

○
○
○
○
○

11 FRIDAY

12 SATURDAY

13 SUNDAY

Palm Sunday

NOTES

"I believe that if you'll just stand up and go, life will open up for you. Something just motivates you to keep moving." – Tina Turner

2025
APRIL

I AM... POSITIVE AFFIRMATIONS

Su	Mo	Tu	We	Th	Fr	Sa
		1	2	3	4	5
6	7	8	9	10	11	12
13	14	15	16	17	18	19
20	21	22	23	24	25	26
27	28	29	30			

April

14 MONDAY

15 TUESDAY

16 WEDNESDAY

17 THURSDAY

GOALS TO COMPLETE

18 FRIDAY

Good Friday

19 SATURDAY

20 SUNDAY

Easter

NOTES

"A life is not important except in the impact it has on other lives." – Jackie Robinson

I AM...

POSITIVE AFFIRMATIONS

April

Su	Mo	Tu	We	Th	Fr
		1	2	3	4
6	7	8	9	10	11
13	14	15	16	17	18
20	21	22	23	24	25
27	28	29	30		

21 MONDAY

22 TUESDAY

Earth Day

23 WEDNESDAY

24 THURSDAY

GOALS TO COMPLETE

25 FRIDAY

26 SATURDAY

27 SUNDAY

NOTES

"If you love life, don't waste time, for time is what life is made up of." – Bruce Lee

2025

KEEP FOCUS ON YOUR DREAMS

MAY

SUN	MON	TUE	WED	THU	FRI	SAT
27	28	29	30	01	02	03
04	05 Cinco de Mayo	06	07	08	09	10
11 Mother's Day	12	13	14	15	16	17
18	19	20	21	22	23	24
25	26 Memorial Day	27	28	29	30	31
01	02					

REMINDERS:

MAY GOALS

HIS MONTH I WANT TO ACCOMPLISH:

HIS MONTH'S GOAL CATEGORY FOCUS:

1	2
3	4
5	6

HOW CAN I IMPROVE:

HABITS TO ESTABLISH:

2025
MAY

I AM...

POSITIVE AFFIRMATIONS

May					
Su	Mo	Tu	We	Th	Fr
				1	2
4	5	6	7	8	9
11	12	13	14	15	16
18	19	20	21	22	23
25	26	27	28	29	30

28 MONDAY

29 TUESDAY

30 WEDNESDAY

01 THURSDAY

GOALS TO COMPLETE

02 FRIDAY

03 SATURDAY

04 SUNDAY

NOTES

"Life is about making an impact, not making an income." – Kevin Kruse

2025 MAY

I AM...

POSITIVE AFFIRMATIONS

May

Su	Mo	Tu	We	Th	Fr
				1	2
4	5	6	7	8	9
11	12	13	14	15	16
18	19	20	21	22	23
25	26	27	28	29	30

05 MONDAY

Cinco de Mayo

06 TUESDAY

07 WEDNESDAY

08 THURSDAY

GOALS TO COMPLETE

- ○
- ○
- ○

9 FRIDAY

10 SATURDAY

11 SUNDAY

Mother's Day

NOTES

"If everything was perfect, you would never learn and you would never grow." –Beyonce

I AM... POSITIVE AFFIRMATIONS

May

Su	Mo	Tu	We	Th	Fr
				1	2
4	5	6	7	8	9
11	12	13	14	15	16
18	19	20	21	22	23
25	26	27	28	29	30

12 MONDAY

13 TUESDAY

14 WEDNESDAY

15 THURSDAY

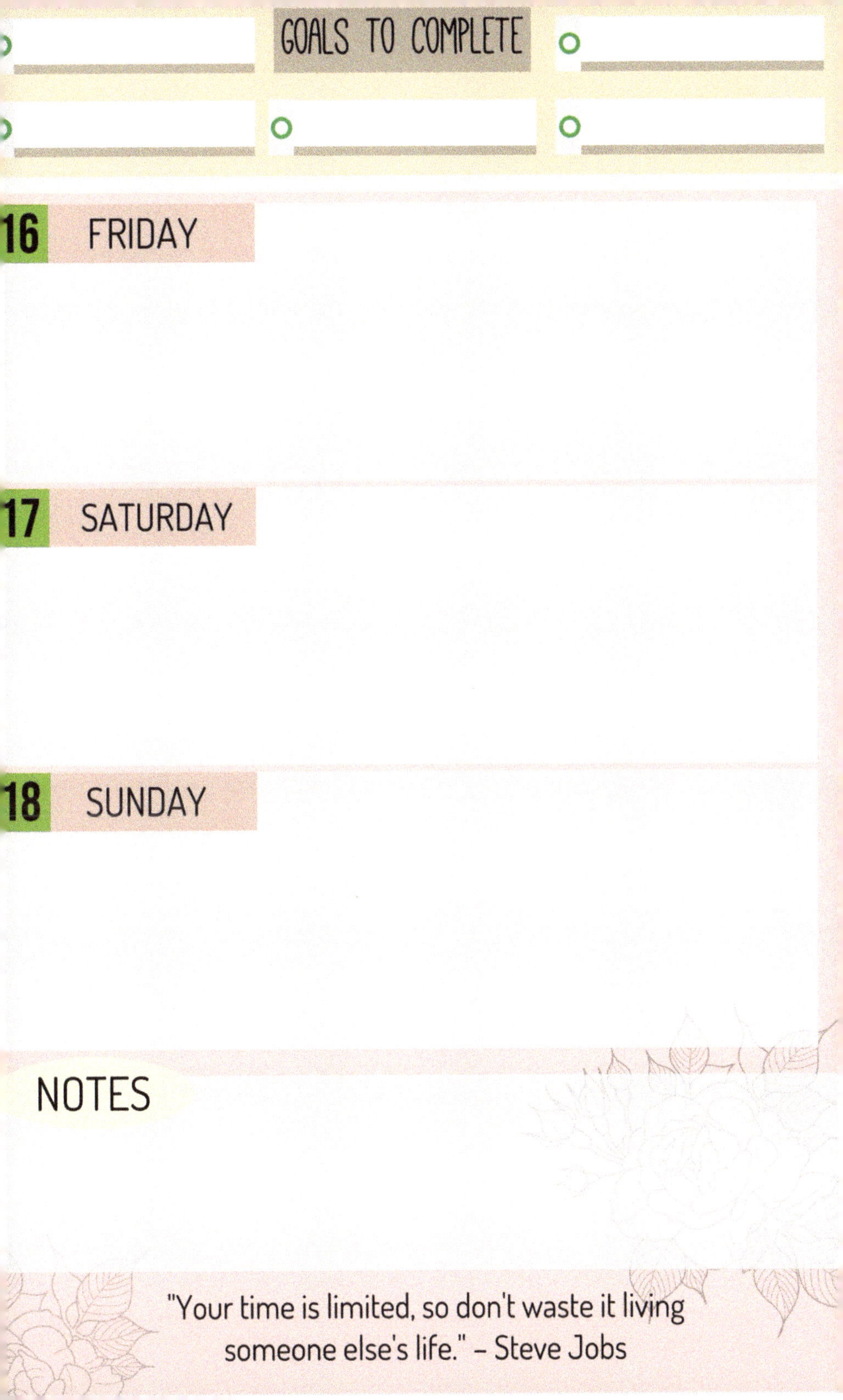

GOALS TO COMPLETE

16 FRIDAY

17 SATURDAY

18 SUNDAY

NOTES

"Your time is limited, so don't waste it living someone else's life." – Steve Jobs

2025
MAY

I AM...

POSITIVE AFFIRMATIONS

May

Su	Mo	Tu	We	Th	Fr
				1	2
4	5	6	7	8	9
11	12	13	14	15	16
18	19	20	21	22	23
25	26	27	28	29	30

19 MONDAY

20 TUESDAY

21 WEDNESDAY

22 THURSDAY

GOALS TO COMPLETE

○

○ ○

23 FRIDAY

24 SATURDAY

25 SUNDAY

NOTES

"Life is very interesting... in the end, some of your greatest pains, become your greatest strengths." – Drew Barrymore

2025 MAY

I AM...

POSITIVE AFFIRMATIONS

May					
Su	Mo	Tu	We	Th	Fr
				1	2
4	5	6	7	8	9
11	12	13	14	15	16
18	19	20	21	22	23
25	26	27	28	29	30

26 MONDAY

Memorial Day

27 TUESDAY

28 WEDNESDAY

29 THURSDAY

GOALS TO COMPLETE

30 FRIDAY

31 SATURDAY

01 SUNDAY

NOTES

"To succeed in life, you need three things: a wishbone, a backbone and a funnybone." – Reba McEntire

2025

WORK HARD, IT WILL PAY OFF

JUNE

SUN	MON	TUE	WED	THU	FRI	SAT
01	02	03	04	05	06	07
08	09	10	11	12	13	14
15 Father's Day	16	17	18	19 Juneteenth	20	21
22	23	24	25	26	27	28
29	30	01	02	03	04	05
06	07					

REMINDERS:

JUNE GOALS

HIS MONTH I WANT TO ACCOMPLISH:

HIS MONTH'S GOAL CATEGORY FOCUS:

1

2

3

4

5

6

HOW CAN I IMPROVE:

HABITS TO ESTABLISH:

2025
JUNE

I AM...

POSITIVE AFFIRMATIONS

June

Su	Mo	Tu	We	Th	Fr
1	2	3	4	5	6
8	9	10	11	12	13
15	16	17	18	19	20
33	23	24	25	26	27
29	30				

02 MONDAY

03 TUESDAY

04 WEDNESDAY

05 THURSDAY

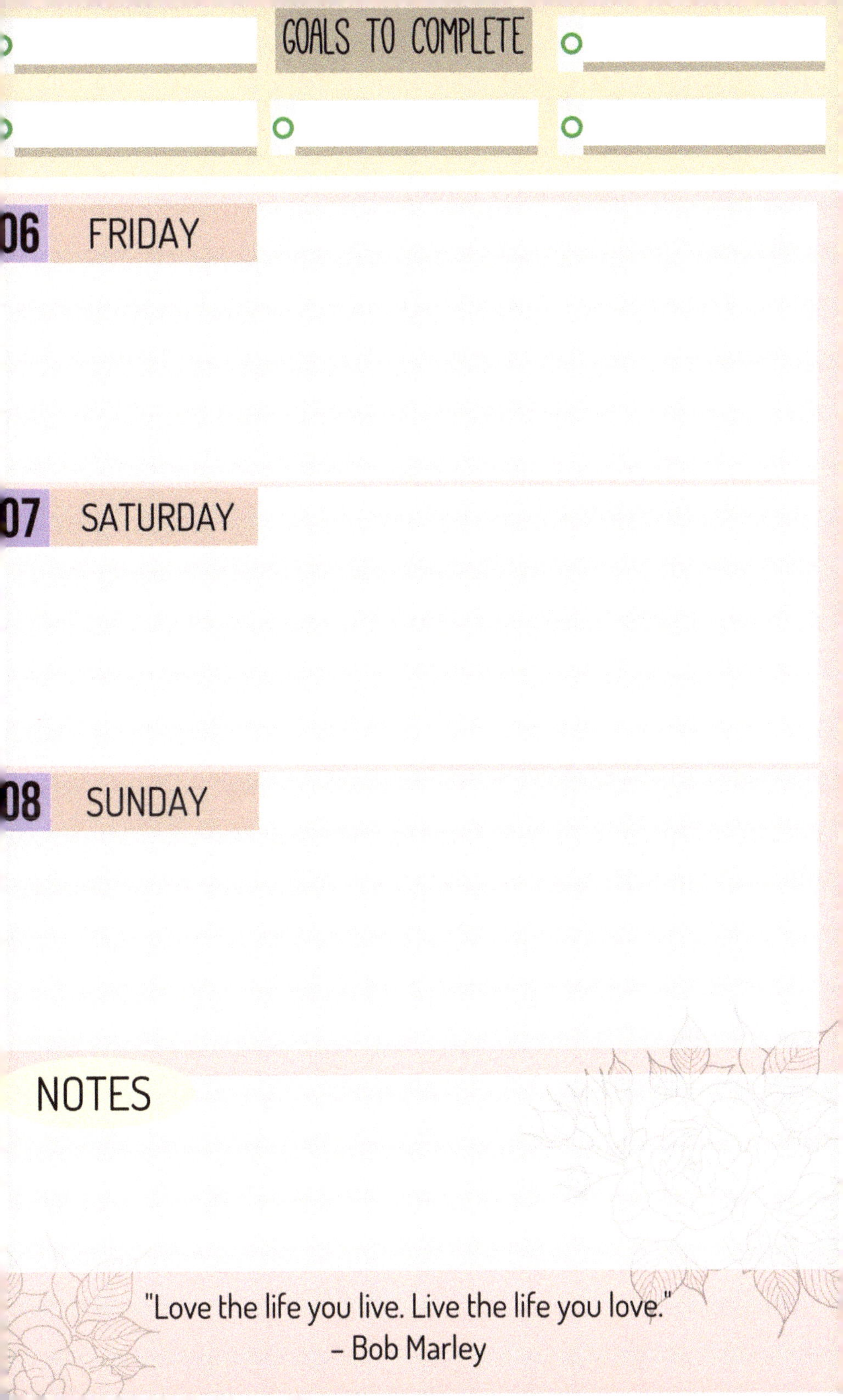

GOALS TO COMPLETE

06 FRIDAY

07 SATURDAY

08 SUNDAY

NOTES

"Love the life you live. Live the life you love."
– Bob Marley

2025 JUNE

I AM...

POSITIVE AFFIRMATIONS

June						
Su	Mo	Tu	We	Th	Fr	Sa
1	2	3	4	5	6	7
8	9	10	11	12	13	14
15	16	17	18	19	20	21
33	23	24	25	26	27	28
29	30					

09 MONDAY

10 TUESDAY

11 WEDNESDAY

12 THURSDAY

GOALS TO COMPLETE

○

○ ○

13 FRIDAY

14 SATURDAY

15 SUNDAY

Father's Day

NOTES

"The whole secret of a successful life is to find out what is one's destiny to do, and then do it." – Henry Ford

2025
JUNE

I AM...

POSITIVE AFFIRMATIONS

June

Su	Mo	Tu	We	Th	Fr
1	2	3	4	5	6
8	9	10	11	12	13
15	16	17	18	19	20
33	23	24	25	26	27
29	30				

16 MONDAY

17 TUESDAY

18 WEDNESDAY

19 THURSDAY

Juneteenth

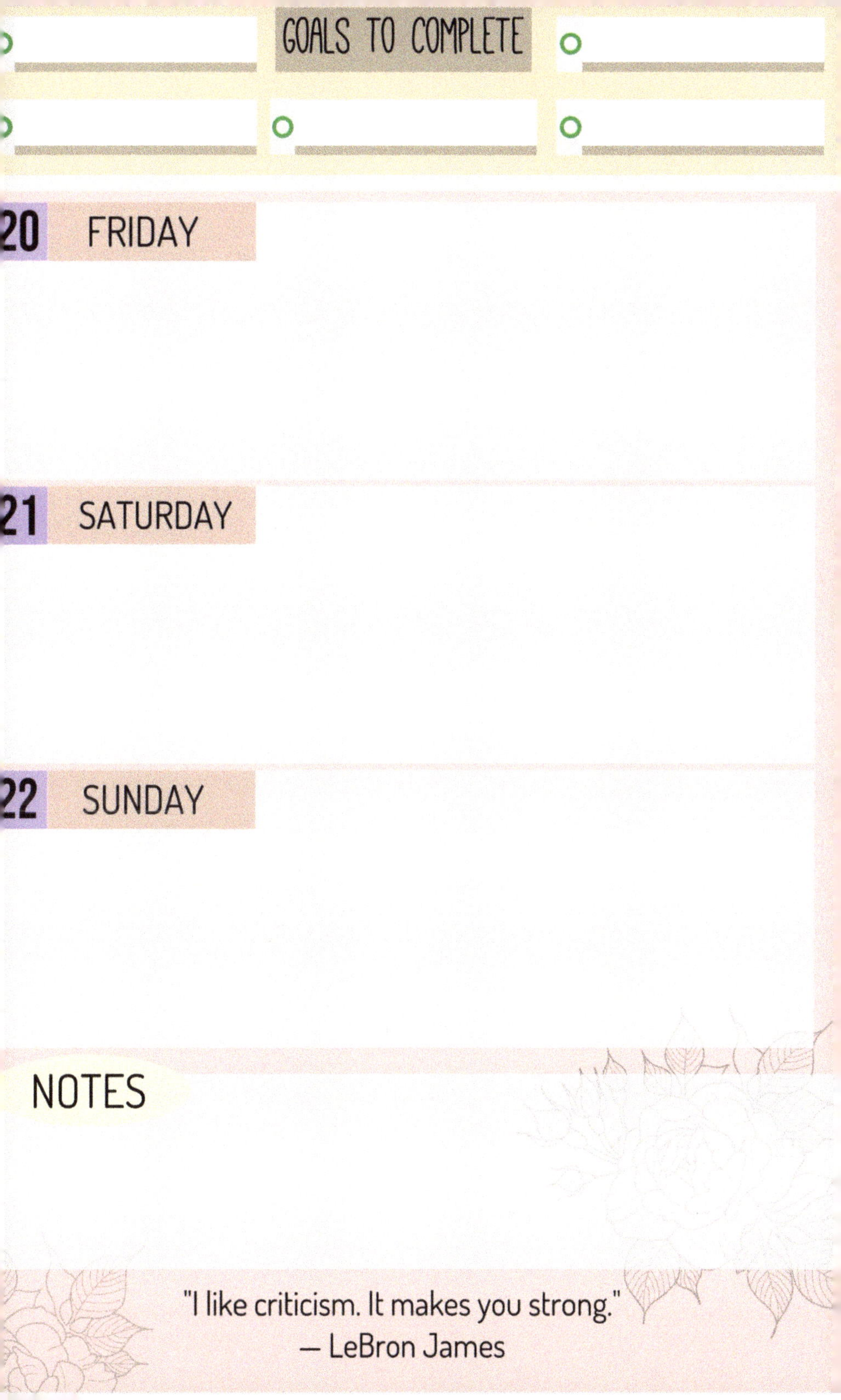

GOALS TO COMPLETE

20 FRIDAY

21 SATURDAY

22 SUNDAY

NOTES

"I like criticism. It makes you strong."
— LeBron James

2025
JUNE

I AM...

POSITIVE AFFIRMATIONS

June						
Su	Mo	Tu	We	Th	Fr	Sa
1	2	3	4	5	6	7
8	9	10	11	12	13	14
15	16	17	18	19	20	21
33	23	24	25	26	27	28
29	30					

23 MONDAY

24 TUESDAY

25 WEDNESDAY

26 THURSDAY

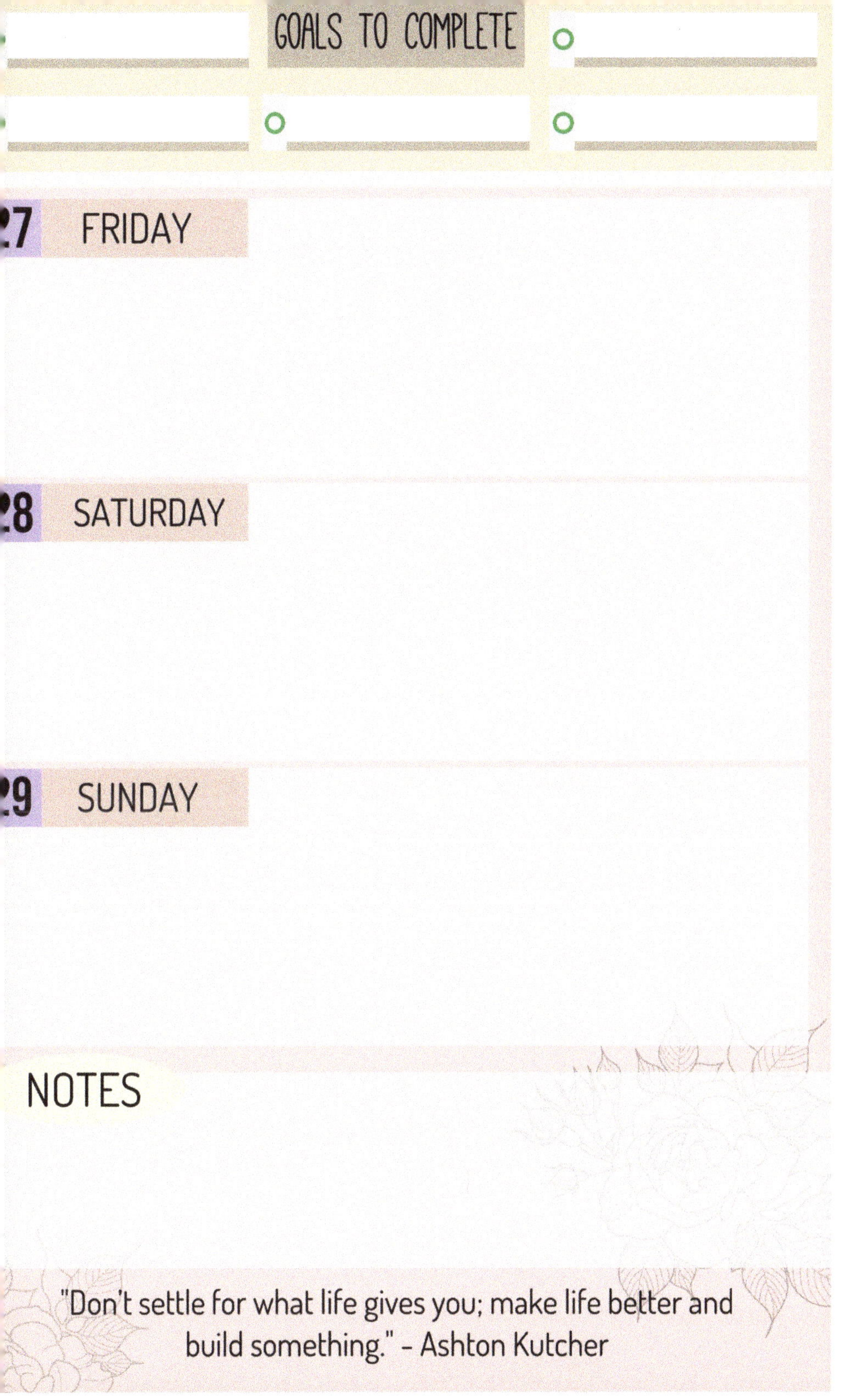
GOALS TO COMPLETE
27 FRIDAY
28 SATURDAY
29 SUNDAY
NOTES
"Don't settle for what life gives you; make life better and build something." - Ashton Kutcher

2025

DON'T LET YOUR GIFTS GO UNNOTICED

JULY

SUN	MON	TUE	WED	THU	FRI	SAT
29	30	01	02	03	04 Independence Day	05
06	07	08	09	10	11	12
13	14	15	16	17	18	19
20	21	22	23	24	25	26
27	28	29	30	31	01	02
03	04					

REMINDERS:

JULY GOALS

THIS MONTH I WANT TO ACCOMPLISH:

THIS MONTH'S GOAL CATEGORY FOCUS:

1

2

3

4

5

6

HOW CAN I IMPROVE:

HABITS TO ESTABLISH:

I AM...

POSITIVE AFFIRMATIONS

July						
Su	Mo	Tu	We	Th	Fr	Sa
		1	2	3	4	5
6	7	8	9	10	11	12
13	14	15	16	17	18	19
20	21	22	23	24	25	26
27	28	29	30	31		

30 MONDAY

01 TUESDAY

02 WEDNESDAY

03 THURSDAY

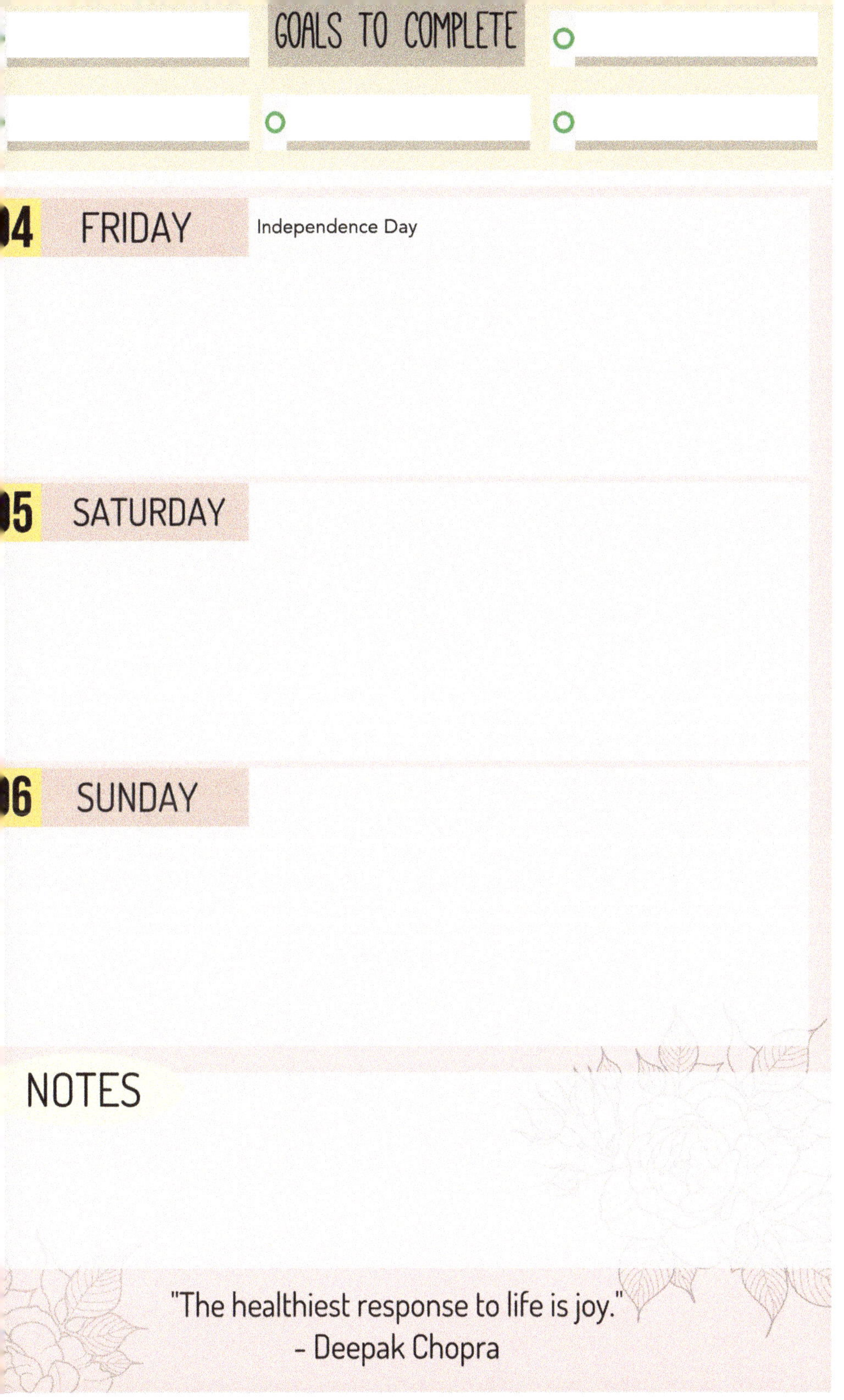

GOALS TO COMPLETE

04 FRIDAY

Independence Day

05 SATURDAY

06 SUNDAY

NOTES

"The healthiest response to life is joy."
- Deepak Chopra

2025
JULY

I AM...

POSITIVE AFFIRMATIONS

Su	Mo	Tu	We	Th	Fr
		1	2	3	4
6	7	8	9	10	11
13	14	15	16	17	18
20	21	22	23	24	25
27	28	29	30	31	

July

07 MONDAY

08 TUESDAY

09 WEDNESDAY

10 THURSDAY

GOALS TO COMPLETE

- ○
- ○
- ○
- ○
- ○

11 FRIDAY

12 SATURDAY

13 SUNDAY

NOTES

"Life is ten percent what happens to you and ninety percent how you respond to it." – Charles Swindoll

2025
JULY

I AM...

POSITIVE AFFIRMATIONS

Su	Mo	Tu	We	Th	Fr	Sa
		1	2	3	4	5
6	7	8	9	10	11	12
13	14	15	16	17	18	19
20	21	22	23	24	25	26
27	28	29	30	31		

July

14 MONDAY

15 TUESDAY

16 WEDNESDAY

17 THURSDAY

GOALS TO COMPLETE

○

○

○

8 FRIDAY

19 SATURDAY

20 SUNDAY

NOTES

"Keep smiling, because life is a beautiful thing and there's so much to smile about." - Marilyn Monroe

I AM...

POSITIVE AFFIRMATIONS

July

Su	Mo	Tu	We	Th	Fr
		1	2	3	4
6	7	8	9	10	11
13	14	15	16	17	18
20	21	22	23	24	25
27	28	29	30	31	

21 MONDAY

22 TUESDAY

23 WEDNESDAY

24 THURSDAY

GOALS TO COMPLETE

25 FRIDAY

26 SATURDAY

27 SUNDAY

NOTES

"Every strike brings me closer to the next home run." - Babe Ruth

2025
JULY

I AM...

POSITIVE AFFIRMATIONS

July						
Su	Mo	Tu	We	Th	Fr	Sa
		1	2	3	4	5
6	7	8	9	10	11	12
13	14	15	16	17	18	19
20	21	22	23	24	25	26
27	28	29	30	31		

28 MONDAY

29 TUESDAY

30 WEDNESDAY

31 THURSDAY

GOALS TO COMPLETE

1 FRIDAY

2 SATURDAY

3 SUNDAY

NOTES

"Too many of us are not living our dreams because we are living our fears." - Les Brown

2025

KEEP STRIVING TO BE YOUR GREATEST

AUGUST

SUN	MON	TUE	WED	THU	FRI	SAT
27	28	29	30	31	01	02
03	04	05	06	07	08	09
10	11	12	13	14	15	16
17	18	19	20	21	22	23
24	25	26	27	28	29	30
31	01					

REMINDERS:

AUGUST GOALS

HIS MONTH I WANT TO ACCOMPLISH:

HIS MONTH'S GOAL CATEGORY FOCUS:

1

2

3

4

5

6

HOW CAN I IMPROVE:

HABITS TO ESTABLISH:

2025
AUGUST

I AM...

POSITIVE AFFIRMATIONS

August						
Su	Mo	Tu	We	Th	Fr	Sa
					1	2
3	4	5	6	7	8	9
10	11	12	13	14	15	16
17	18	19	20	21	22	23
24	25	26	27	28	29	30
31						

04 MONDAY

05 TUESDAY

06 WEDNESDAY

07 THURSDAY

GOALS TO COMPLETE

○

○

○

8 FRIDAY

9 SATURDAY

10 SUNDAY

NOTES

"If you spend your whole life waiting for the storm, you'll never enjoy the sunshine." -Morris West

I AM...

POSITIVE AFFIRMATIONS

August

Su	Mo	Tu	We	Th	Fr
					1
3	4	5	6	7	8
10	11	12	13	14	15
17	18	19	20	21	22
24	25	26	27	28	29
31					

11 MONDAY

12 TUESDAY

13 WEDNESDAY

14 THURSDAY

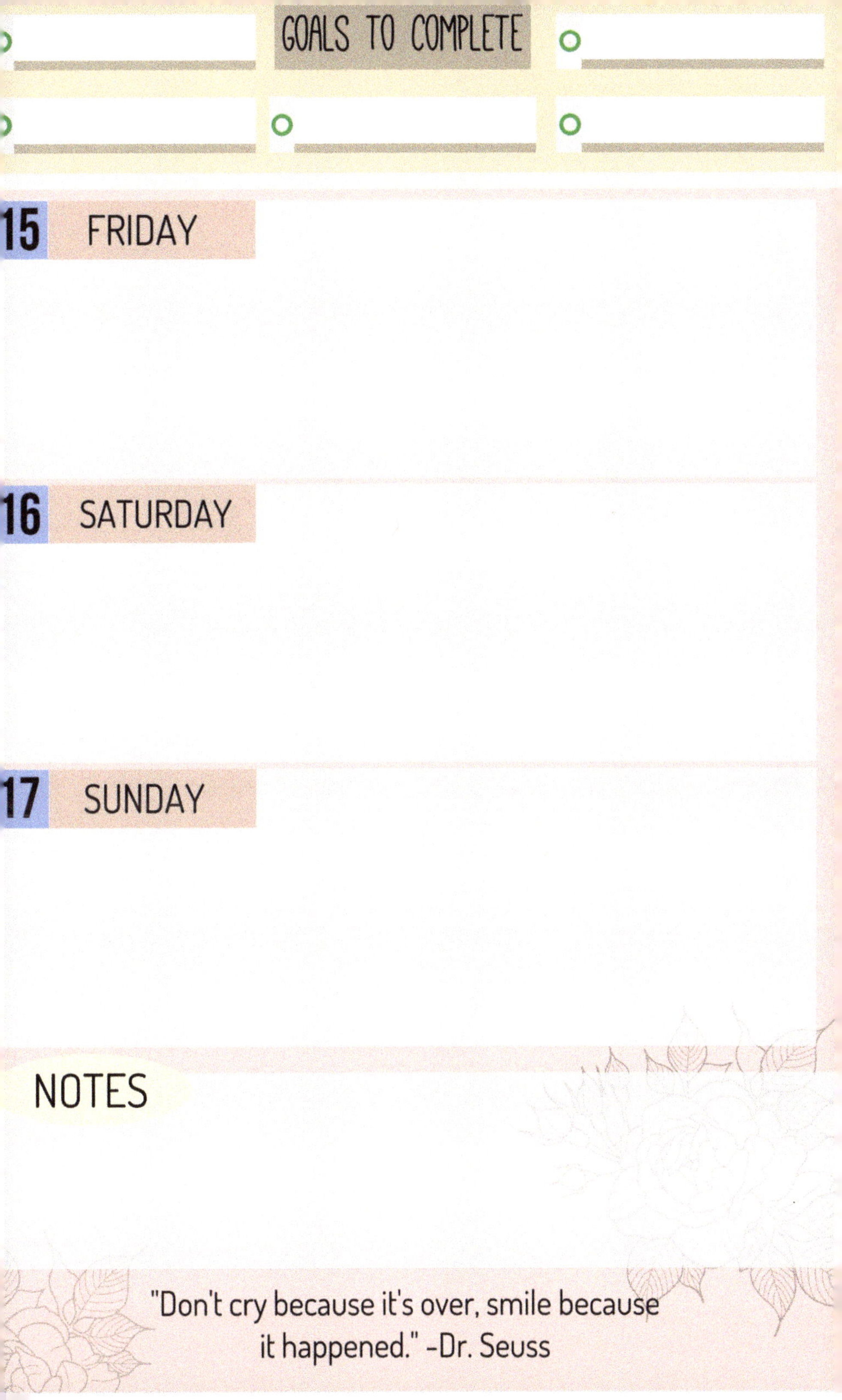
GOALS TO COMPLETE
15 FRIDAY
16 SATURDAY
17 SUNDAY
NOTES
"Don't cry because it's over, smile because
it happened." -Dr. Seuss

2025 AUGUST

I AM...

POSITIVE AFFIRMATIONS

August						
Su	Mo	Tu	We	Th	Fr	Sa
					1	2
3	4	5	6	7	8	9
10	11	12	13	14	15	16
17	18	19	20	21	22	23
24	25	26	27	28	29	30
31						

18 MONDAY

19 TUESDAY

20 WEDNESDAY

21 THURSDAY

GOALS TO COMPLETE

- ○
- ○
- ○

22 FRIDAY

23 SATURDAY

24 SUNDAY

NOTES

"You must expect great things of yourself before you can do them." -Michael Jordan

2025 AUGUST

I AM...

POSITIVE AFFIRMATIONS

August

Su	Mo	Tu	We	Th	Fr
					1
3	4	5	6	7	8
10	11	12	13	14	15
17	18	19	20	21	22
24	25	26	27	28	29
31					

25 MONDAY

26 TUESDAY

27 WEDNESDAY

28 THURSDAY

GOALS TO COMPLETE

- [ ]
- [ ]
- [ ]
- [ ]
- [ ]

29 FRIDAY

30 SATURDAY

31 SUNDAY

NOTES

"When it is obvious that goals can't be reached, don't adjust the goals, but adjust the action steps." -Confucius

2025

YOU ARE CAPABLE OF MORE THAN YOU THINK

SEPTEMBER

SUN	MON	TUE	WED	THU	FRI	SAT
31	01 Labor Day	02	03	04	05	06
07	08	09	10	11	12	13
14	15	16	17	18	19	20
21	22	23	24	25	26	27
28	29	30	01	02	03	04
05	06					

REMINDERS:

SEPTEMBER GOALS

HIS MONTH I WANT TO ACCOMPLISH:

HIS MONTH'S GOAL CATEGORY FOCUS:

2

4

6

HOW CAN I IMPROVE:

HABITS TO ESTABLISH:

2025 SEPTEMBER

I AM...

POSITIVE AFFIRMATIONS

September

Su	Mo	Tu	We	Th	Fr
	1	2	3	4	5
7	8	9	10	11	12
14	15	16	17	18	19
21	22	23	24	25	26
28	29	30			

01 MONDAY

Labor Day

02 TUESDAY

03 WEDNESDAY

04 THURSDAY

GOALS TO COMPLETE

○

○

○

○

○

05 FRIDAY

06 SATURDAY

07 SUNDAY

NOTES

"I guess it comes down to a simple choice, really. Get busy living or get busy dying." -Shawshank Redemption

2025 SEPTEMBER

I AM...

POSITIVE AFFIRMATIONS

September

Su	Mo	Tu	We	Th	Fr
	1	2	3	4	5
7	8	9	10	11	12
14	15	16	17	18	19
21	22	23	24	25	26
28	29	30			

08 MONDAY

09 TUESDAY

10 WEDNESDAY

11 THURSDAY

GOALS TO COMPLETE

○

○ ○

12 FRIDAY

13 SATURDAY

14 SUNDAY

NOTES

"When we strive to become better than we are, everything around us becomes better too." -Paulo Coelho

2025 SEPTEMBER

I AM...

POSITIVE AFFIRMATIONS

September					
Su	Mo	Tu	We	Th	Fr
	1	2	3	4	5
7	8	9	10	11	12
14	15	16	17	18	19
21	22	23	24	25	26
28	29	30			

15 MONDAY

16 TUESDAY

17 WEDNESDAY

18 THURSDAY

GOALS TO COMPLETE

19 FRIDAY

20 SATURDAY

21 SUNDAY

NOTES

"In the long run, the sharpest weapon of all is a kind and gentle spirit." -Anne Frank

2025
SEPTEMBER

I AM...

POSITIVE AFFIRMATIONS

September

Su	Mo	Tu	We	Th	Fr	Sa
	1	2	3	4	5	6
7	8	9	10	11	12	13
14	15	16	17	18	19	20
21	22	23	24	25	26	27
28	29	30				

22 MONDAY

23 TUESDAY

24 WEDNESDAY

25 THURSDAY

GOALS TO COMPLETE

26 FRIDAY

27 SATURDAY

28 SUNDAY

NOTES

"Nothing is more honorable than a grateful heart."
-Seneca

2025

KEEP CONSISTENT.
YOU'LL GO FAR!

OCTOBER

SUN	MON	TUE	WED	THU	FRI	SAT
28	29	30	01	02	03	04
05	06	07	08	09	10	11
12	13 Columbus Day	14	15	16	17	18
19	20	21	22	23	24	25
26	27	28	29	30	31 Halloween	01
02	03					

REMINDERS:

OCTOBER GOALS

HIS MONTH I WANT TO ACCOMPLISH:

HIS MONTH'S GOAL CATEGORY FOCUS:

1

2

3

4

5

6

HOW CAN I IMPROVE:

HABITS TO ESTABLISH:

2025
OCTOBER

I AM...

POSITIVE AFFIRMATIONS

October

Su	Mo	Tu	We	Th	Fr
			1	2	3
5	6	7	8	9	10
12	13	14	15	16	17
19	20	21	22	23	24
26	27	28	29	30	31

29 MONDAY

30 TUESDAY

01 WEDNESDAY

02 THURSDAY

GOALS TO COMPLETE

○

○

○

3 FRIDAY

4 SATURDAY

5 SUNDAY

NOTES

"If we don't change, we don't grow. If we don't grow, we aren't really living." - Gail Sheehy

2025 OCTOBER

I AM...

POSITIVE AFFIRMATIONS

October					
Su	Mo	Tu	We	Th	Fr
			1	2	3
5	6	7	8	9	10
12	13	14	15	16	17
19	20	21	22	23	24
26	27	28	29	30	31

06 MONDAY

07 TUESDAY

08 WEDNESDAY

09 THURSDAY

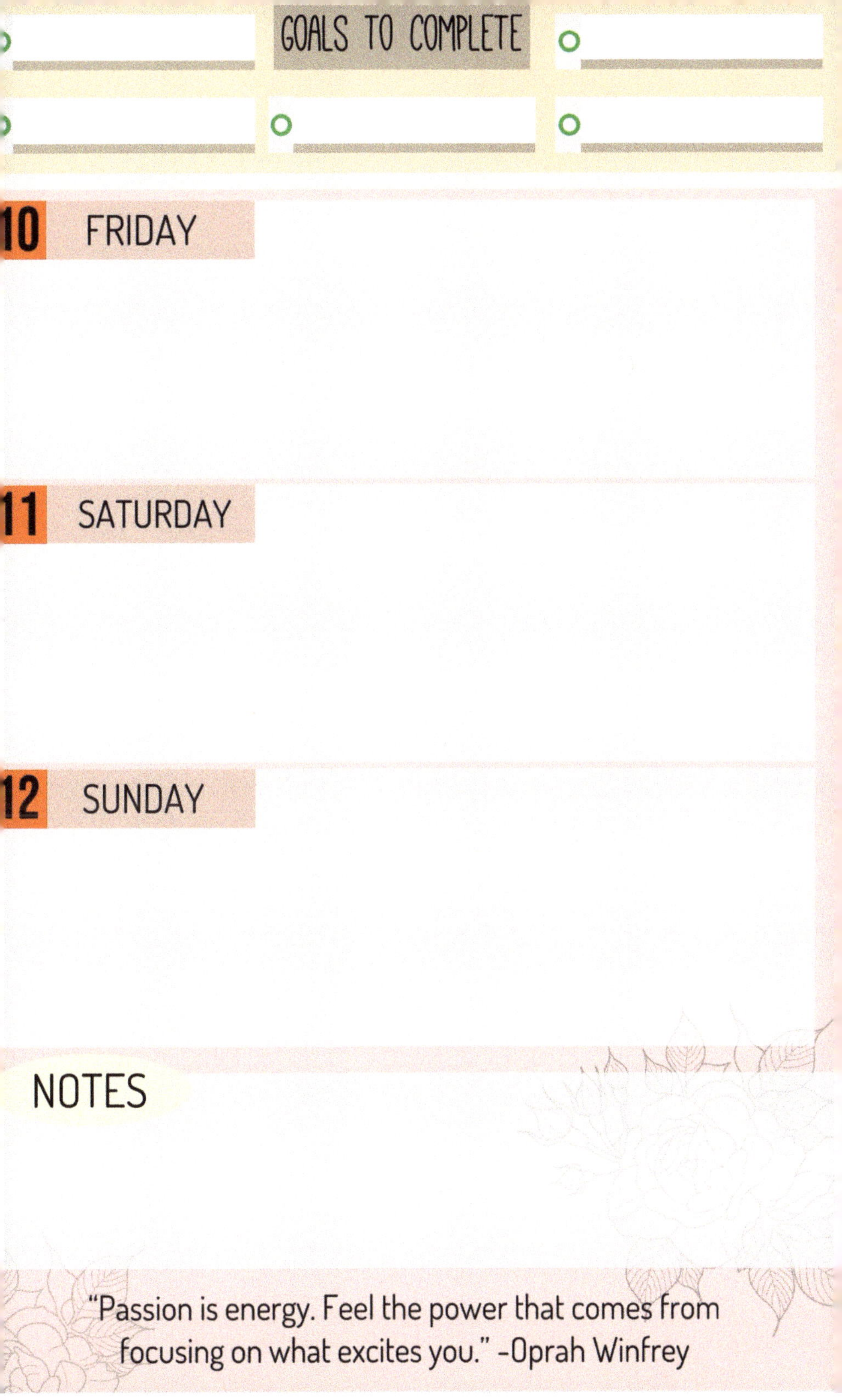

GOALS TO COMPLETE

10 FRIDAY

11 SATURDAY

12 SUNDAY

NOTES

“Passion is energy. Feel the power that comes from focusing on what excites you.” -Oprah Winfrey

2025 OCTOBER

I AM...

POSITIVE AFFIRMATIONS

October						
Su	Mo	Tu	We	Th	Fr	Sa
			1	2	3	4
5	6	7	8	9	10	11
12	13	14	15	16	17	18
19	20	21	22	23	24	25
26	27	28	29	30	31	

13 MONDAY

Columbus Day

14 TUESDAY

15 WEDNESDAY

16 THURSDAY

GOALS TO COMPLETE

○

○

○

7 FRIDAY

8 SATURDAY

9 SUNDAY

NOTES

"I choose to make the rest of my life the best of my life." – Louise Hay

2025 OCTOBER

I AM...

POSITIVE AFFIRMATIONS

October					
Su	Mo	Tu	We	Th	Fr
			1	2	3
5	6	7	8	9	10
12	13	14	15	16	17
19	20	21	22	23	24
26	27	28	29	30	31

20 MONDAY

21 TUESDAY

22 WEDNESDAY

23 THURSDAY

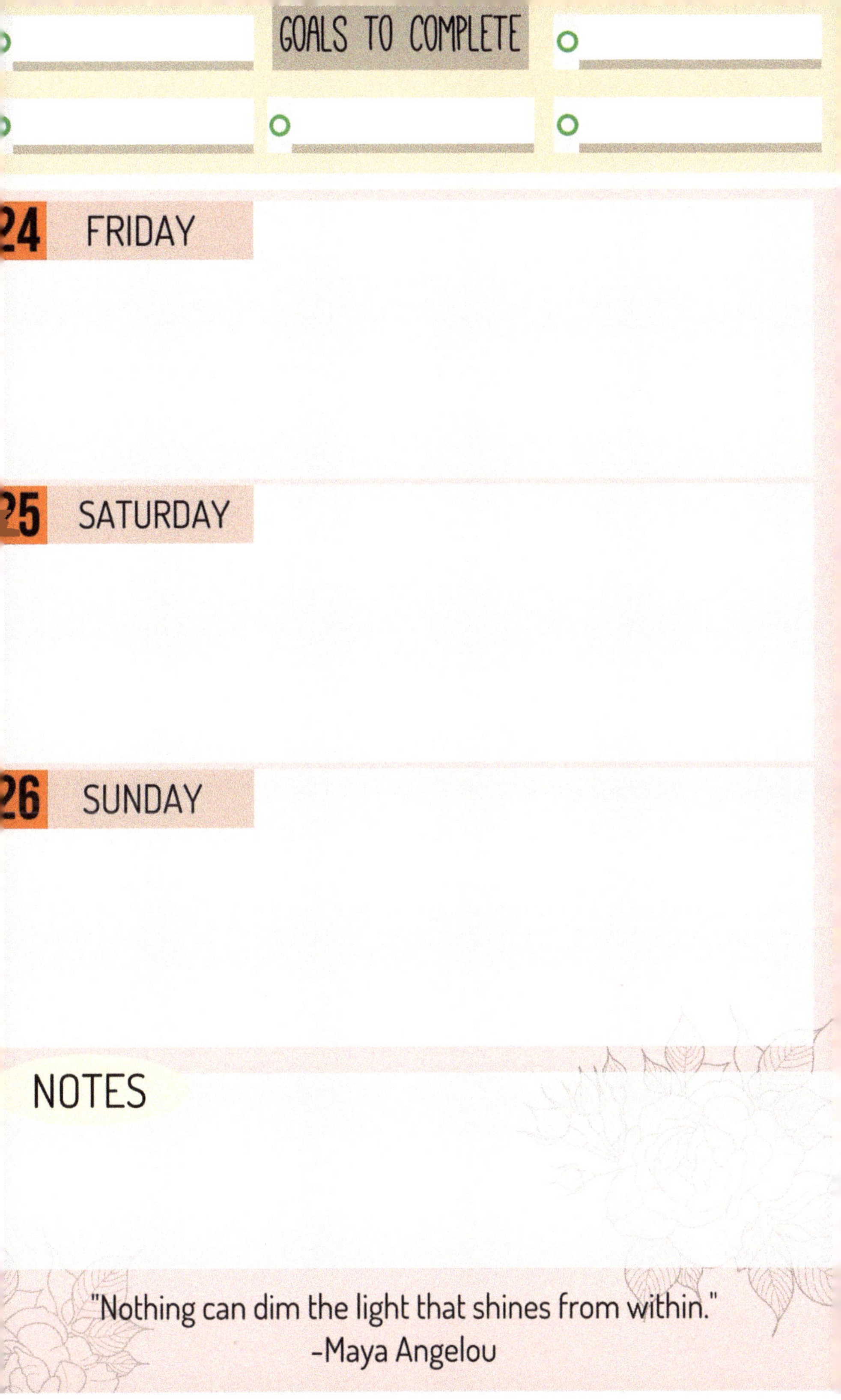

GOALS TO COMPLETE

24 FRIDAY

25 SATURDAY

26 SUNDAY

NOTES

"Nothing can dim the light that shines from within."
-Maya Angelou

2025
OCTOBER

I AM...

POSITIVE AFFIRMATIONS

October

Su	Mo	Tu	We	Th	Fr	Sa
			1	2	3	4
5	6	7	8	9	10	11
12	13	14	15	16	17	18
19	20	21	22	23	24	25
26	27	28	29	30	31	

27 MONDAY

28 TUESDAY

29 WEDNESDAY

30 THURSDAY

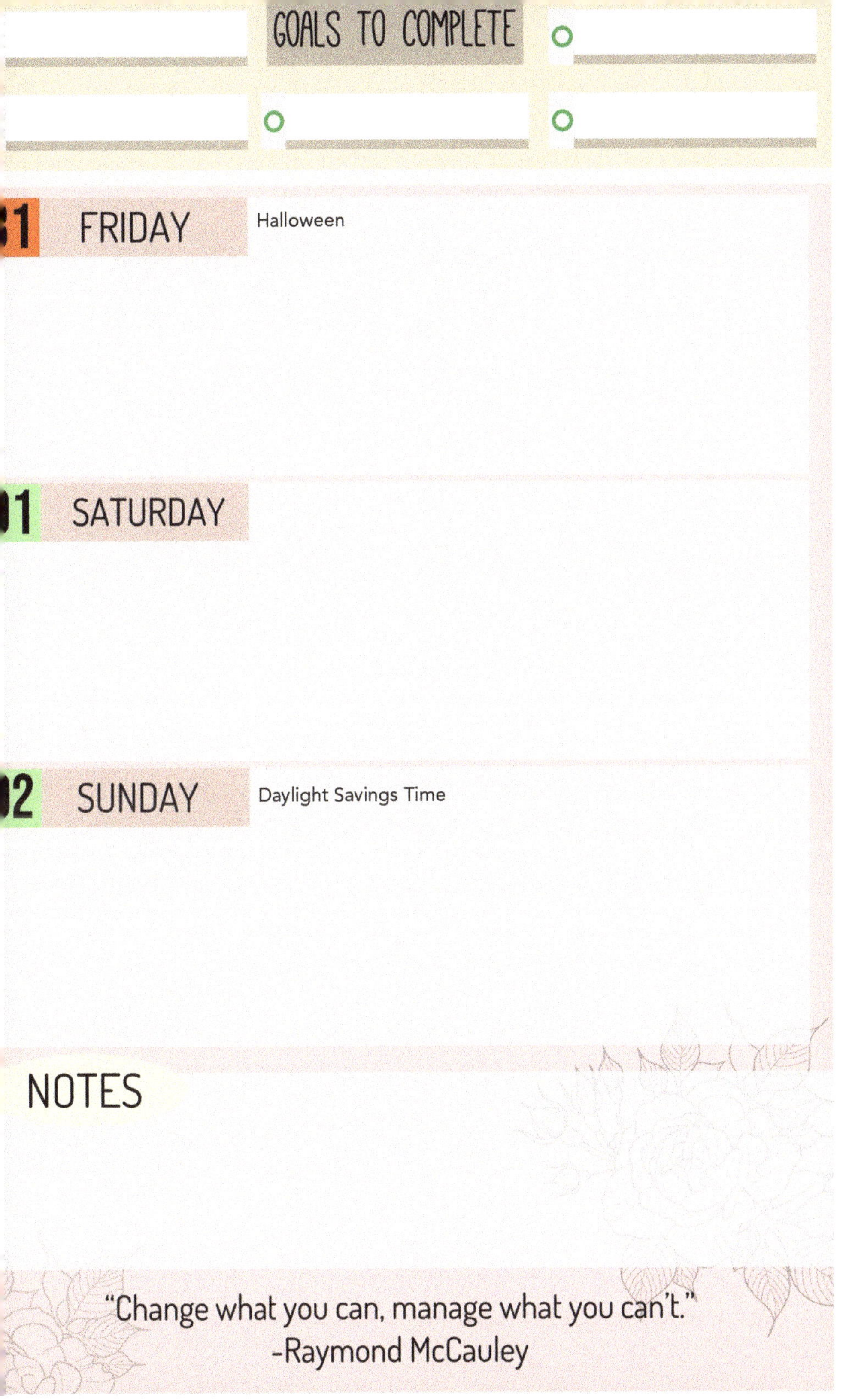

GOALS TO COMPLETE

31 FRIDAY

Halloween

01 SATURDAY

02 SUNDAY

Daylight Savings Time

NOTES

"Change what you can, manage what you can't."
-Raymond McCauley

2025

BELIEVE IN YOURSELF WHEN NO ONE BELIEVES IN YOU

NOVEMBER

SUN	MON	TUE	WED	THU	FRI	SAT
26	27	28	29	30	31	01
02 Daylight Savings Time	03	04	05	06	07	08
09	10	11 Veteran's Day	12	13	14	15
16	17	18	19	20	21	22
23	24	25	26	27 Thanksgiving	28	29
30	01					

REMINDERS:

NOVEMBER GOALS

HIS MONTH I WANT TO ACCOMPLISH:

HIS MONTH'S GOAL CATEGORY FOCUS:

1

2

3

4

5

6

HOW CAN I IMPROVE:

HABITS TO ESTABLISH:

2025
NOVEMBER

I AM...

POSITIVE AFFIRMATIONS

November

Su	Mo	Tu	We	Th	Fr	S
						1
2	3	4	5	6	7	8
9	10	11	12	13	14	
16	17	18	19	20	21	
23	24	25	26	27	28	
30						

03 MONDAY

04 TUESDAY

05 WEDNESDAY

06 THURSDAY

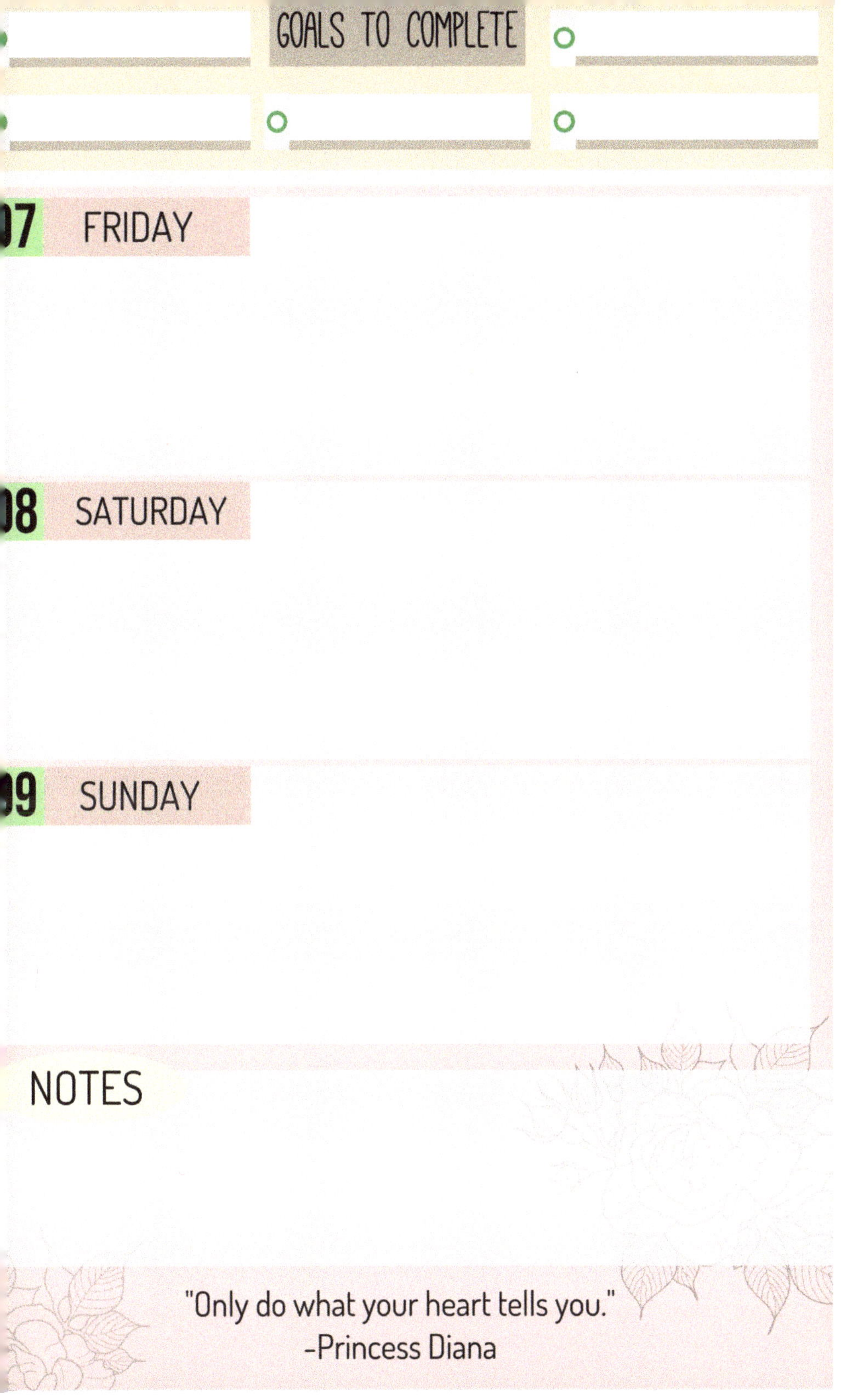

GOALS TO COMPLETE

07 FRIDAY

08 SATURDAY

09 SUNDAY

NOTES

"Only do what your heart tells you."
-Princess Diana

2025 NOVEMBER

I AM...

POSITIVE AFFIRMATIONS

November

Su	Mo	Tu	We	Th	Fr
2	3	4	5	6	7
9	10	11	12	13	14
16	17	18	19	20	21
23	24	25	26	27	28
30					

10 MONDAY

11 TUESDAY

Veteran's Day

12 WEDNESDAY

13 THURSDAY

GOALS TO COMPLETE

14 FRIDAY

15 SATURDAY

16 SUNDAY

NOTES

"Have the courage to follow your heart and intuition. They somehow know what you truly want to become." -Steve Jobs

2025 NOVEMBER

I AM...

POSITIVE AFFIRMATIONS

November						
Su	Mo	Tu	We	Th	Fr	Sa
						1
2	3	4	5	6	7	8
9	10	11	12	13	14	15
16	17	18	19	20	21	22
23	24	25	26	27	28	29
30						

17 MONDAY

18 TUESDAY

19 WEDNESDAY

20 THURSDAY

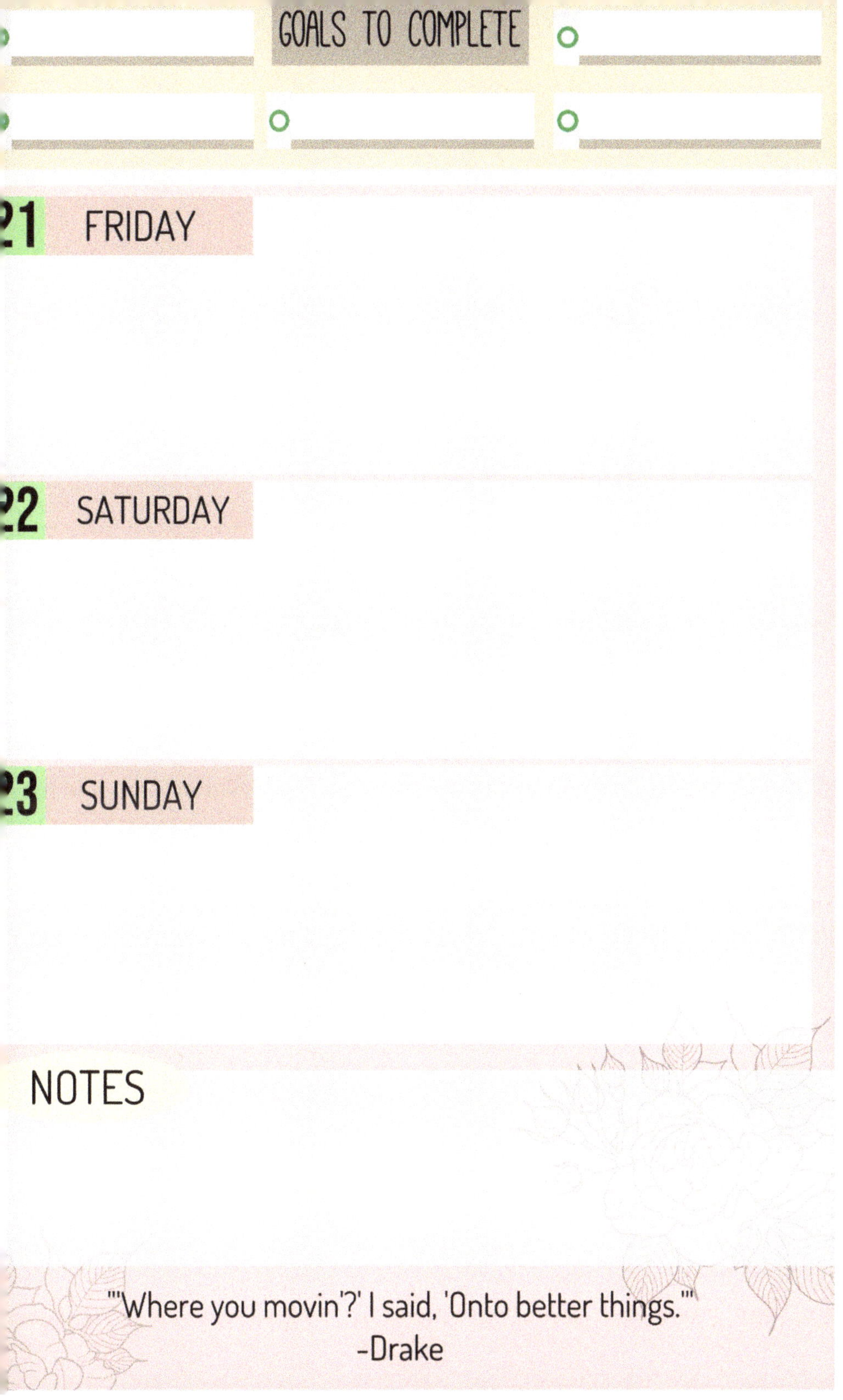
GOALS TO COMPLETE
21 FRIDAY
22 SATURDAY
23 SUNDAY
NOTES
"'Where you movin'?' I said, 'Onto better things.'"
-Drake

2025 NOVEMBER

I AM...

POSITIVE AFFIRMATIONS

November					
Su	Mo	Tu	We	Th	Fr
2	3	4	5	6	7
9	10	11	12	13	14
16	17	18	19	20	21
23	24	25	26	27	28
30					

24 MONDAY

25 TUESDAY

26 WEDNESDAY

27 THURSDAY

Thanksgiving

GOALS TO COMPLETE

28 FRIDAY

29 SATURDAY

30 SUNDAY

NOTES

"Better to live one year as a tiger, than a hundred as a sheep." -Madonna

2025

CHASE THE DREAM
SET IN YOUR HEART

DECEMBER

SUN	MON	TUE	WED	THU	FRI	SAT
30	01	02	03	04	05	06
07	08	09	10	11	12	13
14	15 Hanukkah	16	17	18	19	20
21	22	23	24 Christmas Eve	25 Christmas	26 Kwanzaa	27
28	29	30	31 New Year's Eve	01	02	03
04	05					

REMINDERS:

DECEMBER GOALS

HIS MONTH I WANT TO ACCOMPLISH:

HIS MONTH'S GOAL CATEGORY FOCUS:

2

4

6

HOW CAN I IMPROVE:

HABITS TO ESTABLISH:

2025 DECEMBER

I AM... POSITIVE AFFIRMATIONS

December

Su	Mo	Tu	We	Th	Fr
	1	2	3	4	5
7	8	9	10	11	12
14	15	16	17	18	19
21	22	23	24	25	26
28	29	30	31		

01 MONDAY

02 TUESDAY

03 WEDNESDAY

04 THURSDAY

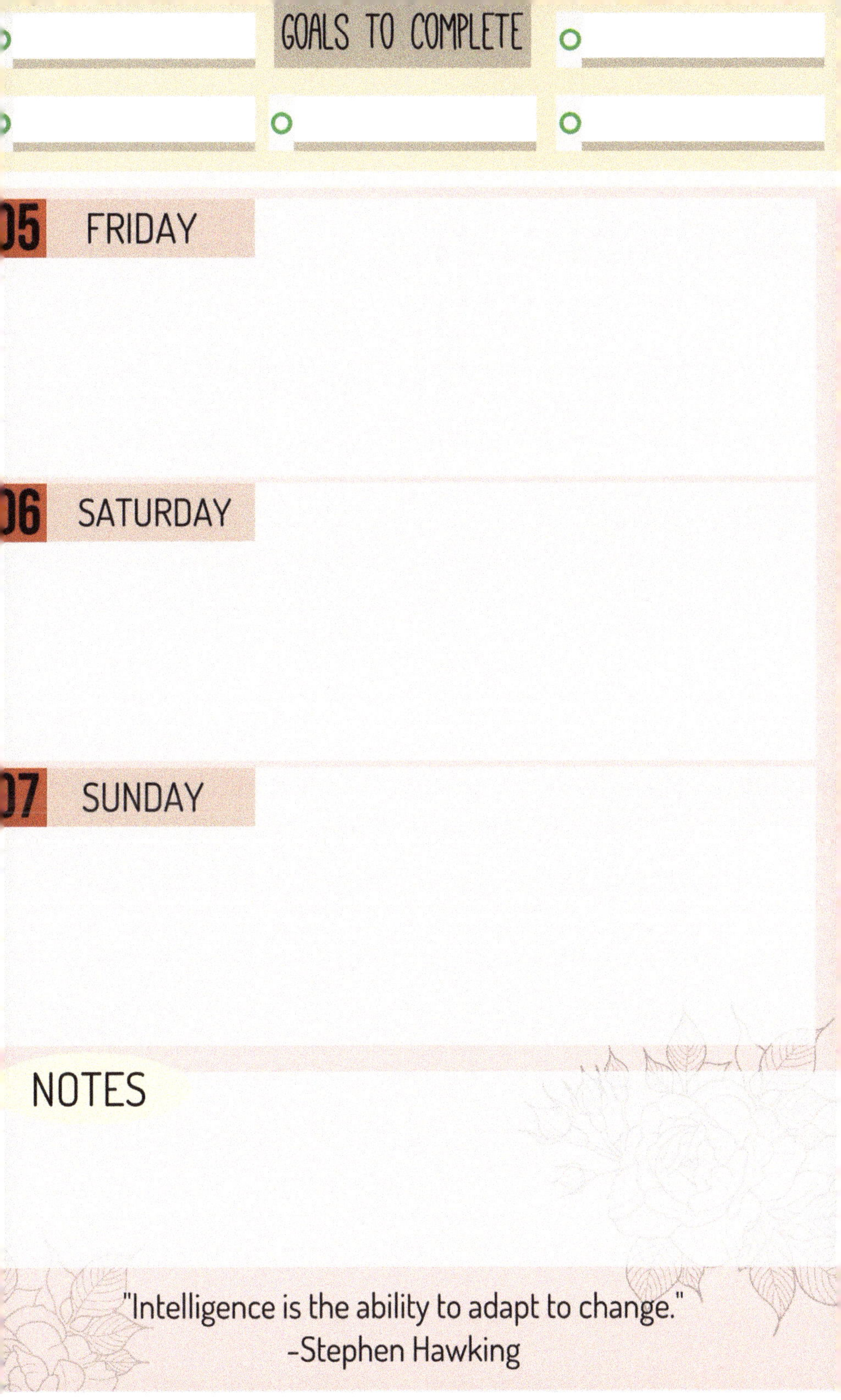

GOALS TO COMPLETE

05 FRIDAY

06 SATURDAY

07 SUNDAY

NOTES

"Intelligence is the ability to adapt to change."
-Stephen Hawking

2025
DECEMBER

I AM...

POSITIVE AFFIRMATIONS

December

Su	Mo	Tu	We	Th	Fr
	1	2	3	4	5
7	8	9	10	11	12
14	15	16	17	18	19
21	22	23	24	25	26
28	29	30	31		

08 MONDAY

09 TUESDAY

10 WEDNESDAY

11 THURSDAY

GOALS TO COMPLETE

12 FRIDAY

13 SATURDAY

14 SUNDAY

NOTES

"Do not allow people to dim your shine because they are blinded. Tell them to put some sunglasses on." -Lady Gaga

2025 DECEMBER

I AM...

POSITIVE AFFIRMATIONS

December					
Su	Mo	Tu	We	Th	Fr
	1	2	3	4	5
7	8	9	10	11	12
14	15	16	17	18	19
21	22	23	24	25	26
28	29	30	31		

15 MONDAY

Hanukkah

16 TUESDAY

17 WEDNESDAY

18 THURSDAY

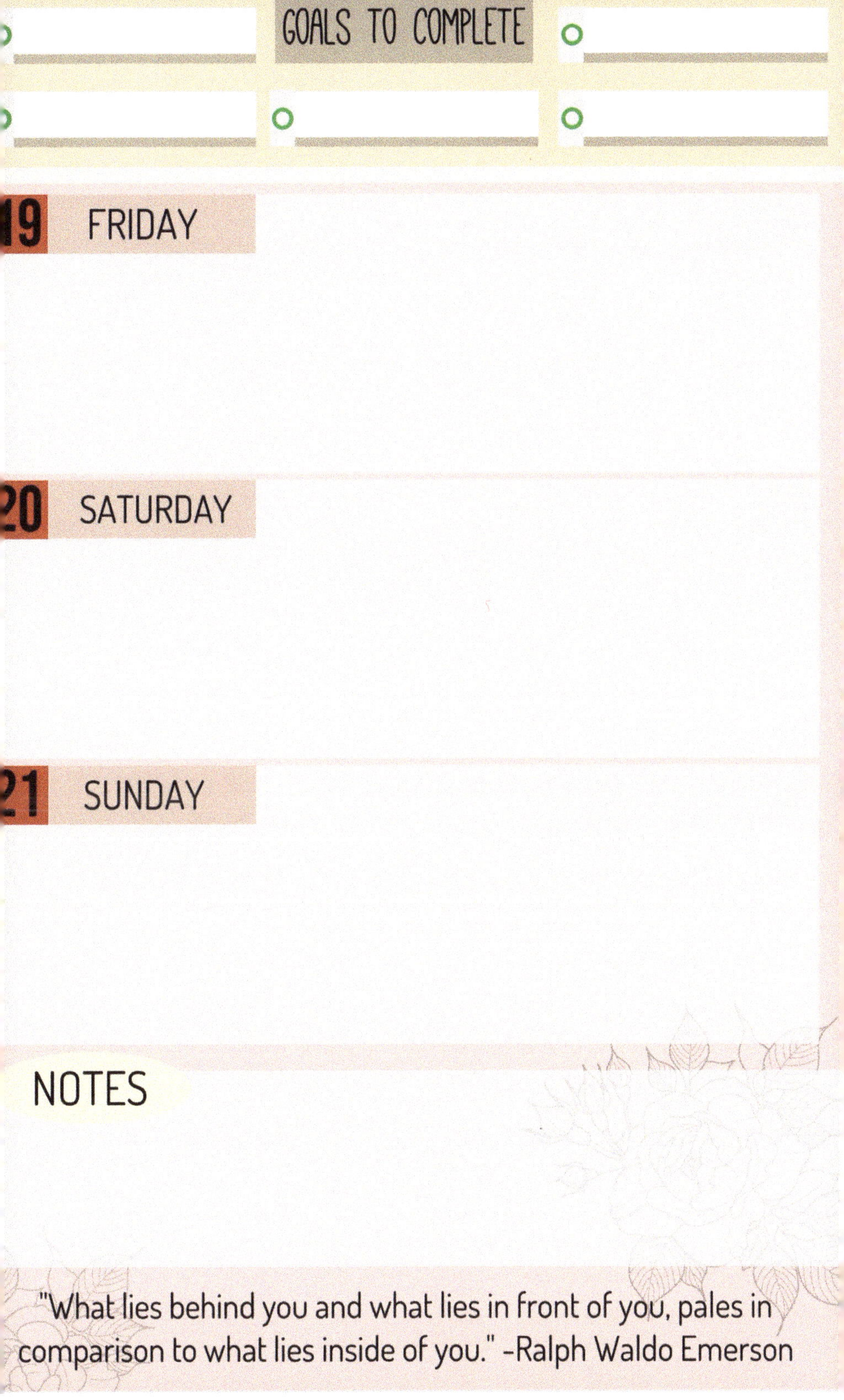

GOALS TO COMPLETE

19 FRIDAY

20 SATURDAY

21 SUNDAY

NOTES

"What lies behind you and what lies in front of you, pales in comparison to what lies inside of you." -Ralph Waldo Emerson

2025 DECEMBER

I AM...

POSITIVE AFFIRMATIONS

December						
Su	Mo	Tu	We	Th	Fr	S
	1	2	3	4	5	
7	8	9	10	11	12	
14	15	16	17	18	19	
21	22	23	24	25	26	
28	29	30	31			

22 MONDAY

23 TUESDAY

24 WEDNESDAY

Christmas Eve

25 THURSDAY

Christmas

GOALS TO COMPLETE

26 FRIDAY

Kwanzaa

27 SATURDAY

28 SUNDAY

NOTES

"Don't try to lessen yourself for the world; let the world catch up to you." -Beyoncé

2025 DECEMBER

I AM...

POSITIVE AFFIRMATIONS

December

Su	Mo	Tu	We	Th	Fr
	1	2	3	4	5
7	8	9	10	11	12
14	15	16	17	18	19
21	22	23	24	25	26
28	29	30	31		

29 MONDAY

30 TUESDAY

31 WEDNESDAY New Year's Eve

01 THURSDAY New Year's Day

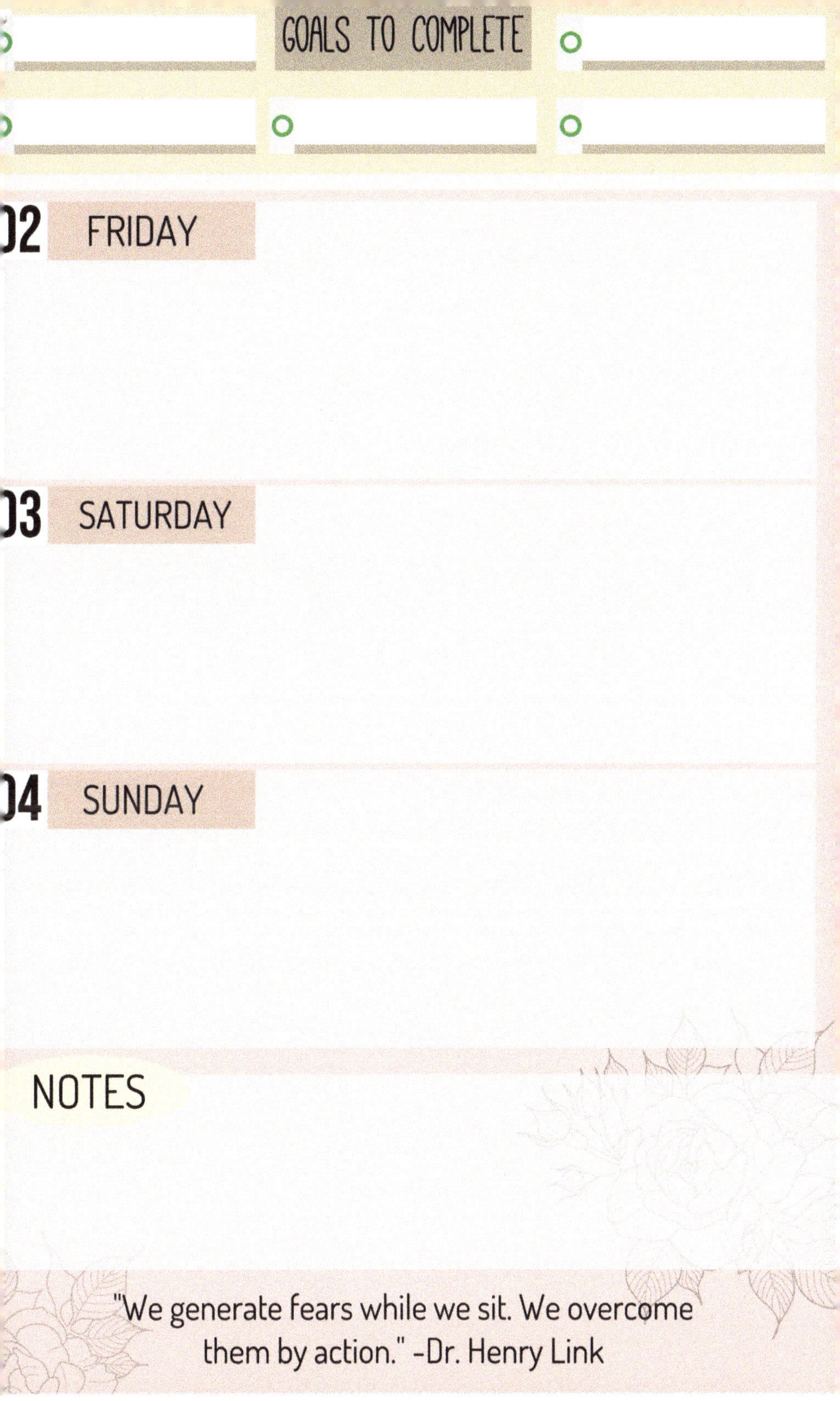

GOALS TO COMPLETE

02 FRIDAY

03 SATURDAY

04 SUNDAY

NOTES

"We generate fears while we sit. We overcome them by action." -Dr. Henry Link

NOTES:

BECOME A LEGACY FOR ALL TO REMEMBER